Laughing Matters

Laughing Matters

The Paradox of Comedy

Scott Cutler Shershow

The University of Massachusetts Press

Amherst   1986

Copyright © 1984 by Scott Cutler Shershow
© 1986 by The University of Massachusetts Press
All rights reserved
Printed in the United States of America
Designed by Barbara Werden
Set in Linoterm Sabon at the
University of Massachusetts Press
Printed by Cushing-Malloy, Inc. and
bound by John Dekker & Sons
Library of Congress Cataloging-in-Publication Data
Shershow, Scott Cutler, 1953–
Laughing matters.
Bibliography: p.
Includes index.
1. Comedy—History and criticism. 2. Comic, The.
I. Title.
PN1922.S54   1986   809'.917   85-16506
ISBN 0–87023–509–5 (alk. paper)

To my parents
who first taught me
what matters

Contents

Preface

If you grew up in America, you probably know about the epitaph of W. C. Fields, but you may know only one of its two versions. Some people will tell you that Fields's gravestone reads "On the whole, I'd rather be in Philadelphia." This piece of gallows humor has become a familiar expression of resignation in the face of the inevitable; even President Reagan echoed it after his brush with death and a ludicrous, lovesick assassin. Some people insist, however, that Fields's gravestone reads, instead, "I'd rather be here than in Philadelphia." The joke makes sense either way, but the change of just a few words produces a quite different comic effect. In the first version, a comedian who had ridiculed the city of brotherly love as a weary, stale, flat, and unprofitable place, finally affirms, like Achilles in the underworld, that life in any shape or location is preferable to its only alternative. In the second version, even death cannot stifle Fields's limitless cynicism about cities and situations, and the comedian goes down fighting, proclaiming to the end that anything is better than some towns.

In fact, neither line is really carved on Fields's gravestone; there are just the usual name and dates. Nevertheless, the two versions of this imagined epitaph together suggest something of the varieties and possibilities of the comic impulse. In these two related jokes, cynicism and optimism, derision and affirmation, join in a kind of paradox where each contradictory emotion is equally powerful, equally comprehensible, and equally funny. This book examines the similar paradoxes of meaning and interpretation that confront us on every level of theatrical comedy. In its content and its conditions alike, comedy on the stage has been, throughout its long history, an on-going dialogue between different moral and social beliefs, different attitudes toward life, death, society, and the human condition. We shall see at more length how the same genre, the same work, even the same joke, can be both generous and cruel, both fierce and forgiving, both radical and reactionary, depending on the play's point of view and our point of view toward the play. These contradictions are part of our enjoyment of comedy, and they have set their imprint on the comic tradition and its critics.

Throughout this book, I am assuming that plays must be understood in their own social context, but that they also contain what Ernst Bloch called a "cultural surplus," a familiar tone or texture that links them together in the pure experience of laughter. Like our two epitaphs—which seem to have fulfilled Satan's boast and created themselves, assuming an existence wholly independent of the actual comedian—comedy speaks to us both from inside and from outside history, an ever-changing mixture of ancient traditions and satire à la mode. Last night's monologue by Johnny Carson, like some of Aristophanes' obscurer choruses, is untranslatable and ephemeral. Falstaff and Chaplin, like their fellow braggart soldiers and crafty servants, endure as familiar images invulnerable to time and linguistic variation. Comedy lives both in puns and in mime, in the turn of phrase and in the raised eyebrow. It is both the most and the least universal of all forms of literature.

Thus this book, like comedy itself, deals in first impressions and second guesses, in broad comparisons and subtle contrasts. The first section looks at plot and character, the basic building blocks of comic plays. We will find, in the confident assertions of classical and neoclassical criticism, a series of interlocking and symmetrical contradictions reflecting the ambiguous "realism" of comic drama. These contradictions define and constitute the paradox of comedy, which proves to be not just a question of theatrical technique and structure, but also a reflection of our own uncertainties about life, society, and ourselves. The second and third sections look at some of the high points of the on-going comic dialogue, some of those magical and paradoxical moments when we confront our past and future in entertainment, and recognize ourselves in the changing but familiar comic mirror. Bypassing many of the best-known comedies, I will look at a selection of plays and playwrights that exemplify the opposing possibilities of the comic spirit. These playwrights indulge us with malice and with love, both mocking and forgiving us our inconsistencies. The tone and purpose of these comedies range from unreasonable cynicism to unreasonable optimism, from absolute irony to absolute faith. Accordingly, the rhythm of *this but also that* will be as characteristic of this book as it is of comedy itself.

Over many years of study and laughter, I have been fortunate in the teachers and friends who have shared their time and insights with me. Among many others, I want to thank Anne Barton of New College, Oxford, who will recognize her influence on this book even at this distance of time; and William Alfred and Robert Chapman of Harvard, who challenged my assumptions, informed my choices, and encouraged my progress, while this book took shape. I am also grateful to Richard Martin, Pam Wilkinson, and their colleagues at the University of Massachusetts Press for bringing the book into the world. And I want to thank, finally, my wife, Karen, for proofreading, for listening, and for everything else.

Needham, Massachusetts
June 1985

One

Comedy and Criticism:

An Ambivalent Tradition

1 Character

> The funniest thing about comedy is that you
> never know why people laugh. I know *what*
> makes them laugh, but trying to get your hands
> on the *why* of it is like trying to pick an eel out of
> a tub of water.
>
> W. C. FIELDS

 The image that W. C. Fields used to describe comedy itself had been used many centuries earlier by Plautus in describing one of those typical slaves whose schemes provided a framework and a focus for Roman New Comedy. "What happens when he is caught in the act?" someone asks about this particular slave. The answer is simple: "He slips away like an eel."[1] As comedians and critics alike suggest, the study of comedy often comes to resemble its object. Henri Bergson could be describing a Plautine slave when he observes that comedy "has a knack of baffling every effort, of slipping away and escaping only to bob up again."[2] Sigmund Freud calls a similar character to our minds when he describes a joke as "a double-dealing rascal who serves two masters at once."[3] From the classical comic mask to George Meredith's satyrlike "comic spirit," the idea of comedy seems always to take on human shape. Critics turn toward metaphor in a doomed effort to define the indefinable, but in the end, all jokes wiggle free from definition, turning the very act of analysis into one more incongruity.

There is an odd sense of relief or triumph in this conclusion. As our metaphors suggest, comedy is elusive, slippery, and subject to what could be called an "uncertainty principle" because measurement transforms or destroys it. But this very fact seems somehow flattering to our humanity. It pleases us that we cannot explain the "sense of humor" we all (or nearly all) possess. Critics of comedy invariably begin with an apology, and in the heart of every commentator is a certain regret that, in this case at least, all criticism destroys its object. As Freud put it, "if one laughs at a joke really heartily, one is not in precisely the best mood for analyzing its technique."[4] Still, even this observation is a kind of witticism, and our knowing smiles suggest which side we are really on in the war between comedy and criticism.

Ingeniously enough, Freud himself takes the conflict between enjoying and analyzing a joke as the starting point for a theory of laughter. He argues, in terms that have now become familiar, that the techniques of comedy are unconscious strategies to circumvent our rational conscience. We are of two minds about our hard-earned reality principle, and in comedy we manage both to flatter it and to expose its limitations. Jokes that Freud calls "innocent," with their surprises and incongruities, their puns and wordplay, allow us to insult reason by a luxurious indulgence in nonsense, but give reason the final victory by exposing whatever logical error or fallacy is involved—by "getting" the joke. In more complex jokes, the kind that really makes us laugh, Freud postulates a relationship between what he calls the "joke-work" and the "tendentious" message that the joke communicates, an opposition not unlike the familiar literary distinction between form and content. As Freud describes it, each of these two sides of a complex joke serves as a disguise for the other. The tendentious material diverts our conscious attention from the prerational, infantile joy we take in the nonsense and the wordplay, while these verbal elements distance our conscious minds from the violence and aggression that jokes so often express. It is in this sense that jokes are "double-dealing," and express our deep ambivalence toward life itself, our infantile greed for disorder, and our emotional hesitation about the forms and institutions of adult society. Freud thus makes explicit a general point that is implicit in the whole history of comic theory: comedy is always something larger, deeper, and more complicated than it seems. The way in which we disguise the emotions expressed in jokes is as important as the emotions themselves. As everyone occasionally notices, a joke that too nakedly expresses hostility or aggression is not really very funny. It is unforgivable to forget the "punch line," but it is even worse to refer to a particular joke *by* its punch line, thus making a complete telling of it impossible. In jokes, as so often in life, getting there is half the fun. If this too is a sort of witticism, it is one that resonates with complications to which we shall have to return.

Freud's study represents an appropriate culmination to the general philosophic tradition of comic theory, for the focus of that tradition has often tended toward the psychological. The striking physical manifestations of the comic spirit—those "violent convulsions of the face and sides," that "ugly and distorted" yet not painful expression of both the classical comic mask and the laughing human face—have always invited analysis of the psychic factors that produce them.[5] But the focus must broaden in turning from the specific comic utterance to the fully realized stage comedy, from the individual psyche to that community of author, actor, and audience that is the comic theater. A comedy on the stage may obviously contain individual jokes, humorous characters, and comic situations. Usually a comedy is funny and makes its audiences laugh, although at least one study warns us, in all solemnity, not to consider this affective response to be an intrinsic aspect of the genre.[6] But funny or not, we recognize certain conventions of structure and content without which a play cannot seem, in the normal sense, a comedy. In a complex and on-going historical process, these conventions enter into our experience of comic drama, acting upon performers and spectators alike; and part of our enjoyment of comedy springs from the intricate fulfillment of our conventionalized expectations.

Classical and neoclassical criticism of comedy, a tradition beginning with Plato and Aristotle, accelerating in late antiquity and extending through the Renaissance and beyond, has examined the comedies of a handful of dramatists with a pedantic thoroughness that evokes a sense of comic incongruity when compared with its object. There is sometimes a tedious level of general agreement in this critical tradition that preyed endlessly on itself

and for whom certain of the earliest commentators achieved ca-
nonical status. But its specific insights form an overall pattern in
which scholarly consistency disguises hidden conflicts. As they
analyze and describe the nature of comic characters or the structure of comic plots, the classical critics tend to contradict one
another and themselves in neatly symmetrical ways. I will be using
some of these contradictions and symmetries as the starting point
for a newer and probably no less ambivalent approach to the idea
of comedy. In retrospect, the classical critics may seem dogmatic
to the point of madness, stiff with affectations inherited from an
irrelevant past, and comically blind to obvious infidelities or hidden virtue. But maybe their very inconsistencies reflect something
of comedy's influence and power.

In any case, formal critics are only the last in a series of con-
centric circles of auditors and spectators, willing participants in
the comic experience who listen and look, who pay their money
and make their choices. Every comic writer sometimes grumbles
about facing a theater full of amateur critics, and laughter itself is
the final and most absolute critical judgment. But the clashing
theoretical concepts that accompany the comic tradition do
reflect a fundamental ambiguity of theatrical art—which human
beings have always known as both a reflection of social reality and
a living part of that reality. All plays exist, in Leo Salingar's terms,
as both "mirror" and "performance."[7] Comic subjects and comic
audiences are finally the same; comic writers must portray but
also please the world. It is this double nature that makes the long-
debated concept of "dramatic realism" so difficult to identify and
define, particularly with comedy. At once an image of life and a
stylized entertainment, a target of intense scholarship and a popular diversion, comic drama continues to be a powerful expression
of our prejudices and half-articulate beliefs, our instinctual passions and irreversible refinements.

Even the earliest interpretations of comedy must themselves be
interpreted with a rich sense of ambiguity. Comedy, argues Aristotle at the beginning of the critical tradition, "aims at representing men as worse . . . than in actual life," and is "an imitation of
characters of a lower type" (*Poetics* 2.4; 5.1). The phrasing sug-

gests how this deceptively simple formulation could later be explained in terms of social class, even though Aristotle makes clear he is speaking in an ethical sense. The moral agents within the comic "mirror" are "beneath . . . our own level of goodness," below that level of everyday morality we presumably recognize in ourselves. Aristotle's argument assumes a general consensus on ethical values which allows a certain subtlety to the description: comic characters possess some "defect" or "ugliness," though they are not "in the full sense of the word bad" (5.1). Since this is approximately how we all see ourselves, we may find it difficult to distinguish between comedy as thus described and a type of drama that presents characters "as they are" in real life (2.1). Aristotle really seems to be suggesting that the moral average of comic characters is lower; that we may assume we will meet in comedy those defects that we may chance to meet in life.

Aristotle's argument does not imply an analogous condemnation of comedy as "performance." To a modern commentator, the *Poetics* represents a specific defense of the imitative arts intended to answer the harsh criticism of Aristotle's great philosophic rival.[8] Plato's discussion of the drama, conversely, culminates in a profound philosophic rejection of *mimesis* itself, but it begins by assuming, with Aristotle, that comedy portrays those actions that are "unworthy" of a free citizen. The subject matter of comedy, once again, is below the moral norm that Plato expects from his readers, involving "buffooneries" that one should "blush to practice" in real life (*Republic* 10.606c).[9] For Plato, both the content and the process of comic theater are morally degraded and degrading, harmful to the human soul no less than to the health of society. The comic dramatist, absolutely banished from the ideal commonwealth of the *Republic,* is severely restricted even under Plato's later, more practically conceived constitution:

> As for the play of uncomely body and mind and the artistes of ludicrous burlesque in diction, song, dance, and all the characteristic effects of the three . . . we shall enjoin that such representations be left to slaves or hired aliens . . . the

sportive entertainment to which the name *comedy* is universally given may be taken as disposed of on these lines by our law.
(*Laws* 7.816e)[10]

The stern, magisterial tone of passages like these emphasizes what
must have been the vitality and subversive power of ancient
comedy. Even Aristotle, in a nonliterary context, abandons his
mysterious doctrine of *katharsis* with its implication that drama
could have a positive, therapeutic effect on a body of citizens. He
prescribes that "the legislator should not allow youth to be spectators of iambi or of comedy until they are of an age to sit at the
public tables and to drink strong wine; by that time education will
have armed them against the evil influences of such representa-
tions" (*Politics* 7.17).[11] The implied analogy between comedy
and intoxication manages, curiously, to glance backwards at
comedy's patron deity, and forward to a long tradition of religious and moral diatribe. The suspicion about comedy's effect on
society and the individual would influence the later history of
comedy no less than those formal and structural rules that later
playwrights and critics discovered, or believed they discovered, in
the *Poetics*.

For Plato and Aristotle, then, comedy involves characters who
are worse than people ought to be. Aristotle was mostly concerned with the formal content of comic plays, but I would like to
follow Plato and look outside as well as inside the theater in my
consideration of comic literature and its critics. It is striking, for
example, that the same slaves and aliens Plato would choose for
his actors have often been typical figures within the drama. Plato's
dislike of the whole process of playing a part, similarly, points
toward the enduring bohemianism of "theater people" and the
suspicion with which respectable society has so often viewed
them. Formal aspects of the comic mirror, at least as critics describe them, often correspond to aspects of comic performance in
the real world. This, too, is a point to which I shall have reason to
return.

Later critics would more or less agree that the "ridiculous," as
Plato put it, must itself be considered "a certain kind of bad-

ness."[12] Theophrastus, the pupil and successor of Aristotle, actually wrote something called the *Characters*, a group of thumbnail sketches of personality types resembling the *dramatis personae* of plays written by Menander, his own most famous pupil. These lively descriptions of what a later dramatic tradition would call Vices, turn characteristics such as "Boorishness," "Buffoonery," "Flattery," and the like, into fully realized character types. Probably they both reflected and influenced the character types of contemporary comedy. The small fraction of Menander's enormous output that we know, are comedies of manner already revealing what would be a lasting comic interest in the nuances of character and social life. And six of Theophrastus's characters have the same titles as those of lost plays by Menander.[13] Whatever influence the master may have had upon his gifted student would influence in turn the history of comedy on the stage, whose character types continue to betray the influence of Menandrine New Comedy through to the Marx brothers and beyond.

For critics, the types of comic characters that we find first in Greek New Comedy would shift gradually from conventions of dramatic portrayal to full-fledged standards of dramatic realism. The Roman poet Horace had some sensible advice for the playwright who wanted "an approving hearer, one who waits for the curtain." To keep the audience glued to the seats, Horace advises, the characters should speak and act in a manner appropriate to their age and social station (*Ars Poetica* 153–57).[14] With the drama, however, critical principles have a way of expanding past their original intentions almost as much as doctrinal principles in religion. Horace's practical suggestion becomes, with the literary critics of the Renaissance, the formal doctrine of *decorum* which demanded a fidelity to established types of character, oddly enough, in the name of verisimilitude. Aristotle saw the "generalizing" power of later Greek comedy as representing an advance in realism over the topical "lampoons" of the older playwrights (*Poetics* 5:3), and later critics, taking the idea one step further, made the idea of truth-to-type a basic criterion for aesthetic truth in drama. From our own post-Romantic perspective, this is an example of the fundamental ambiguity of theatrical "realism," which, for the critics of the Renaissance, involves an adherence to conventional images of human life rather than any attempt to evoke life's genuine variety and individuality.

The types themselves, both in theory and on the stage, remain persistently associated with vice. To the comic spirit, we are typically corrupt: boys will be boys, and so forth. Here, for example, are four poets and critics repeating a comic litany of misdeeds and loose living, apparently suggesting a consistent view of human nature no less than of comedy:

> you must note the manners of each age, and give a befitting tone to shifting natures and their years. The child . . . flies into a passion and as lightly puts it aside, and changes every hour. The beardless youth . . . soft as wax for moulding to evil, peevish with his counsellors, slow to make needful provision, lavish of money. . . . Many ills encompass an old man . . . sluggish and greedy of a longer life, surly, given to praising the days he spent as a boy, and to reproving and condemning the youth. (Horace, *Ars Poetica* 154–75)

> as long as tricky slave, hard father, treacherous bawd, and wheedling harlot shall be found, Menander will endure. (Ovid, *Amores* 1.15.17–18)[15]

> to work a comedie kindly . . . yonge men should showe the imperfection of youth, Strumpets should be lasciuious, Boyes vnhappy, and Clownes should speake disorderlye. (George Whetstone, dedication to *Promos and Cassandra*, 1578)[16]

> [In comedy] we get as it were an experience, what is to be looked for of a niggardly Demea, of a crafty Davus, of a flattering Gnato, of a vainglorious Thraso. (Sir Philip Sidney, "A Defense of Poetry," c. 1583)[17]

Supposedly eulogizing a playwright or offering practical advice for the making of plays, these passages also convey a familiar assumption of feminine immorality, and a characteristic comic cynicism about the human community in general. Comedies on the stage frequently present us with the same kind of comic litany, reciting the varieties of our prevailing and perennial corruption:

I see all the world is but a Gull . . .
A Marchant to a Courtyer is a Gull:
A clyent to a Lawyer is a Gull:
A marryed man to a Bacheler, a Gull:
All to a poet, or a poet to himself.
(George Chapman, *All Fooles*, 2.1.361–66)[18]

HARCOURT. Most men are the contraries to that they would
    seem. Your bully, you see, is a coward with a long sword; the
    little humbly-fawning physician, with his ebony cane, is he
    that destroys men.
DORILANT. The usurer, a poor rogue, possessed of mouldy
    bonds and mortgages; and we they call spendthrifts, are only
    wealthy, who lay out his money upon daily new searches of
    pleasure.
HORNER. Ay, your arrantest cheat is your trustee or executor;
    your jealous man, the greater cuckold; your churchman, the
    greatest atheist; and your noisy pert rogue of a wit, the great-
    est fop. . . .
(William Wycherley, *The Country Wife*, 1.1)[19]

Whether hypocrite or cynic, to each his own vice. In the world of
comedy, not only are suckers born every minute, but they certainly never get an even break.

Most actual comic plays, of course, do contain characters who
are portrayed as morally good. The Aristophanic *eiron,* for example, was the beginning of a long tradition of comic wits whose
understated good sense would continue to deflate the boors and
buffoons of other stages. Sometimes playwrights would deliberately reverse the conventional moral status of a character type.
But when Terence, for example, portrays a trustworthy and
sympathetic courtesan in his *Mother-in-Law,* it is only an exception that proves how deeply ingrained was the conventional
comic view of women. There is a continuing association between
comedy and vice in many other aspects of comic theory and practice. Consider the claims made by Jonson, Molière, and others
that comedy scourges vice by making it ridiculous; or Jonson's
idea of a comedy of "humour" that focuses on eccentricities of

behavior; or even that conceptual image of comedy as a "double-dealing rascal." In our actual experience of comedy on the stage, we most remember and enjoy the crafty slave and the con man, the imposter and the Vice, or the fat, cowardly drunkard and thief called Falstaff. In the long tradition of Platonic or puritan attacks on the theater, it is comedy, with its buffooneries and its belly laughs, with scandalous behavior both on stage and off, that comes in for most of the abuse.

Of course when we describe comic characters as "worse," we actually mean they are "no better" than in actual life—a paradox that has been implicit throughout my argument. The traditional approach to comic character actually disguises and accompanies the slightly different notion that comedy is, in Cicero's famous phrases, *imitatio vitae, speculum consuetudinis, imago veritatis* (an imitation of life, a mirror of custom, an image of the truth).[20] Comedy degrades the world it depicts, but not beyond recognition. It was equally a convention of classical criticism to contrast the exalted, idealized personages of tragedy with the "low" characters of comedy, and to look to the comic stage for a realistic picture of the way of the world. Horace observes that comedy, taking its subject matter from daily life, demands a particular accuracy of observation (*Epistles* 1.2.168–70). The actions of comedy, in other typical phrases repeated by the Renaissance critics, are "everyday occurrences" and "our private and domestical matters." Thus comic characters are both worse than us and exactly like us, and the comic principle *così fan tutti* (that's the way everyone does it), expresses both a cynical view of human nature and a pretension of dramatic realism. Cynicism in general may be seen either as a negative distortion of reality, or as a simple unillusioned acceptance of the world as it actually is. This ambivalence is also comedy's.

There is one final ambiguity that clings to Aristotle's basic idea throughout its long history. The same Renaissance critics who spent most of their time carefully imitating the ancients eventually managed to change what had been a moral and aesthetic idea into a political one. Aristotle himself refers to the presumed rustic origins of comedy, mentioning a traditional explanation that the earliest comedians were performers who "wandered from village to village, being excluded contemptuously from the city" (*Poetics* 3.3). In the brevity of Aristotle's remarks on the form, as well as in their specific purport, a certain note of condescension is clear: he argues that comedy is the instinctive art form of "the more trivial sort" of people (4.7), and that it "has had no history, because it was not at first taken seriously" (5.2). This might be part of the reason that later poets and critics, paraphrasing Aristotle's formulation about comic characters, invariably interpret it in terms of social class:

> in comedy it is necessary to use jocose acts of persons of low rank and unknown. (Trissino, *Poetica*, 1529)[21]

> Tragedy . . . differs from comedy in the rank of the characters.
>   Comedy employs characters from rustic, or low city life. (Scaliger, *Poetices Libri Septem*, 1561)[22]

> the persons of comedy are of poor spirit and inclined to obey the magistrates and to live under the laws . . . they are in a poor and humble state. (Castelvetro, *Poetica d'Aristotele Vulgarizzata et Sposta*, 1571)[23]

For Dante, his poem was a *commedia* partly because it was written in "the vulgar tongue in which even housewives hold converse."[24] This image of "divine" comedy expressed in plebeian language conveys, once again, a sense of the duplicity of the critical tradition. Aristotle said that comedy was not "at first" taken seriously, but even a contemporary comedian could

> . . . dare to speak before the Athenian people
> About the city in a comic play.
> For what is true even comedy can tell.[25]

And although later critics tried to point the force of comedy at the lower classes, the social vision in any of the best-known works of the comic theater is by no means so simple. Indeed, the typical lower-class characters of comedy are usually portrayed to be of equal or higher moral worth than their "betters." Comic butts, far more often, have been the unsuccessful pretenders to high social rank: the awkward or foppish aristocrat, the middle-class snob, the *bourgeois gentilhomme*. In many great comedies, such as

Shakespeare's, we laugh impartially at the contrast between characters of different rank, and perceive coexistent visions of the uselessness or the inevitability of all social classes. Some critics, including both Sidney and Fielding, insist that real destitution and misery ought never to be the object of ridicule. In so insisting, however, they implicitly affirm that

> *Nil habet infelix paupertas durius in se*
> *Quam quod ridiculos homines facit.*

The worst thing about poverty is that it makes men ridiculous.[26]

As I shall show at more length, these are the persistently ambiguous ideas of societies that were, like their comedies, sometimes divided against themselves.

2   Plot

In 1823, Charles Lamb was writing about the comedy of a previous age with the same mixture of nostalgic appreciation and apology that the Renaissance neoclassicists lavished on Plautus and Terence. Lamb's essay on "the artificial comedy, or Comedy of manners"[1] focuses on a form of comic drama that was later than most of what we discussed in chapter one, but his apposition still proves to be, in the terms of my argument, less simple than it sounds. Traditionally, comedy was realistic precisely because it served as Cicero's "mirror of custom," yet for Lamb, a group of comic writers whose self-announced intention was to mirror the nuances of manner and custom in their society was producing an "artificial" comedy. This is really as much a paradox of life as of drama, because the artificiality that Lamb finds in Restoration comedy refers not so much to its aesthetic character as to the nature of the society that it portrays. As social life itself becomes more complex, we get a comedy of manners, or of mannerisms, whose "realism" is correspondingly artificial. Within a social setting in which theater plays an important role, real people sometimes model their behavior on the theatrical ideal, deepening the paradoxical relationship between drama and life. All these are

issues raised by the development of what is sometimes called "genteel" comedy, which is a form that stands in direct contradiction to the classical image of the genre, and one that will not be a major concern in this essay. Still, it is significant that Lamb precisely inverts the notions of comic character we have considered so far. The classical critics saw comic characters as "worse than in actual life," and yet found a keen sense of reality in the completed comic play. When Lamb argues that the scandalous behavior of Restoration heroes and heroines transpires in a "Utopia of gallantry" where real moral standards need not apply, we see the critical notions of comic character come full circle. Thus Restoration comedy, which formed an amusingly accurate image of the lives and pursuits of its original audience, and whose characters were often based on some of the real men and women who composed and watched it, becomes for the Romantic critic a moral Saturnalia of temporary indulgence, merely the "loose pranks of two hours' duration, and of no after consequence." Lamb's words remind us that the ambiguity of comic character, reaching both away from and toward "reality," is similar to that of the Saturnalia itself—those festivals of license and misrule that recur throughout the folklore of our culture and that, as modern critics have taught us, serve as a symbolic image and pattern in our comedies.[2] In Saturnalian festivity, the human community both distorts and reaffirms the social facts of its life, allowing a temporary period of anarchy which serves as an ironic confirmation of law and order. On the stage, similarly, we ridicule the figures of authority and deny, for the moment, the real relations of power and submission that structure our lives, but we do so with the unspoken acknowledgment that the stage is not the world, that holidays and plays alike must end. "The incompetent judge, the mock doctor," and other such figures are, as Ian Donaldson put it, "the familiar and recurrent figures in the comedy of a society which gives a general assent to the necessity of entrusting power to its governors, judges [and] doctors."[3]

Through its typical characters, then, comedy represents but also distorts the world as we know it, turning toward but also away from the human reality of which the comic spirit itself remains a familiar aspect. Comic plots, even more obviously, reveal the same ambiguous approach to reality. If the first thing we notice about comic characters is their perennial corruption and credulity, the first thing we notice about comic plots is their inevitable optimism. As we have seen, classical critics tended to see the social rank of comic characters as the distinguishing feature of the genre, but in the living practice of comedy, from Menander to the television sitcom, the one absolutely indispensable aspect, the one universally accepted convention, is the happy ending. If all comic endings are not in every sense of the word "happy," virtually all comic plays end on some note of renewal, forgiveness, or simple well-being. Dante, as we have partly seen, addressed the critical notions of both comic characters and comic plots in explaining why his poem ought to be considered a comedy: because it was written in the vulgar tongue of everyday life, and also because "in its beginning it is horrible and foul . . . in its ending, fortunate, desirable and joyful."[4] Some two centuries later, the critic Scaliger would also observe that "the beginning of a comedy presents a confused state of affairs, and this confusion is happily cleared up at the end."[5] The inevitable structure of a comic plot goes from misapprehension to understanding, from separation to reconciliation. The *nodus erroris,* the knot of complications, is unfastened and, usually, a different sort of knot is tied for at least two of the younger characters.

Donatus the Grammarian, an enduring influential fourth-century critic, observes that "In tragedy, life is depicted as something to be shunned; in comedy, as something to be eagerly taken."[6] A modern school of anthropological criticism has taught us more specifically how comedy originated in celebrations of life's seasonal renewal, and how a celebratory sense of the value and continuity of life has remained a persistent quality of comic theater. Comedy glorifies life, however, only by presenting it as more perfect than it really is. The events of comedy work out with dance-like precision and symmetry, in exact contrast to how events work out in the world. In one aspect, comedy conveys the Saturnalian sense of temporary holiday, but in another, comedy portrays a world where one lives "happily *ever after,*" where "Jack shall have Jill / Nought shall go ill."[7] There is an obvious and almost comical symmetry to our argument: comic characters are, to quote Aristotle's formulation one last time, "worse" than in life, but comic plots are "better" than in life—more fortunate, more desirable, more inevitably joyful, than the unpredictable succession of events through which we struggle on the earthly stage.

One of the pleasures of comedy is our certain knowledge that, no matter what the perturbations of the plot, all shall be well. For it is, of course, precisely this knowledge that life denies to us. The last act of a comedy, says Donatus, is the "solution, pleasing to the audience, and made clear to everyone."[8] Aristotle points out that "those who, in the piece, are the deadliest enemies . . . quit the stage as friends at the close, and no one slays or is slain," and that, in all drama, such an ending "is accounted the best because of the weakness of the spectators" (*Poetics* 13.7–8). True enough, people like to see things work out for the characters whose fate has engaged their sympathy and concern. The happy ending is what modern psychologists call "wish fulfilling." In our moments of theatrical respite from the slaughter and enmity of the real world, comedies humor our vulnerability, refusing to admit impediments to the marriage of true minds. The chorus of Ben Jonson's *Magnetic Lady* promises, just before the final act, to "entertain the spectators, with a convenient delight, till some unexpected and new encounter break out to rectify all and make good the conclusion" (4.8.27–31).[9] Here again is the familiar ambiguity: Jonson's conclusion is good in both the moral and aesthetic sense, for it "rectifies" both the characters' lives and the play itself. The comic playwright rewards our hearts, yet also our minds; our affection for the characters, yet also our intellectual perception of the work.

In another sense, these two poles of sympathy and criticism embody the same two approaches to reality that I have found in other aspects of comedy. There seems to be some mysterious dialectic between that willing suspension of disbelief which, as Coleridge accurately observed, is part of our approach to all fiction, and our equally stubborn insistence that fiction retain some fidelity to reality as we know it. As a Renaissance critic put it, the events of comedy must be "taken from the nature and custom of human actions," and yet must be intermingled with "those things which are beyond our hope and expectation."[10] Comedy's "precarious logic," in a modern critic's words, "can tolerate every kind of 'improbability.' "[11] The last-minute reprieve, the long-lost relative, the unexpected inheritance, indeed every variety of happy chance, all are familiar to us from the final moments of numerous plays. Just as characters are often corrupt in the world, but are always corrupt in comedy, so these miraculous events *could* happen in the world, but are expected on the stage, at least by the audience. In practice, comedy sometimes approaches romance, or even its more distant cousin, the fairy tale. All plays portray a significant pattern of human actions and are thus in some sense coincidental; but in comedy, the coincidence is a model of the human condition, "the true and perfect image of life indeed."

The convention of a happy ending clearly means that comedy can never be entirely realistic. But the critics of the classical tradition, starting from an implacable conviction that all drama must be an imitation of life, an image of the truth, apparently felt compelled to stress the verisimilitude of comic resolutions. Here are some other samples from ancient and modern critics, all in basic agreement about the limits of the comic vision of reality:

> The poet . . . constructs the plot on the lines of probability. (Aristotle, *Poetics* 9.5)
>
> Realistic narrative recounts imaginary events which yet could have occurred, like the plots of comedies. (Cicero, *Ad Herrennium*)[12]
>
> [Comedy's] plot comprises only actions possible to happen. (Castelvetro)[13]
>
> The comic catastrophe is commonly the result of much artifice; for, short of violating decorum and verisimilitude, the author must somehow contrive a happy ending. (Marvin Herrick)[14]

As comic characters are corrupt and yet familiar, so comic plots are marvelous and yet plausible. We know from our experience of comedy on the living stage, however, that some of the most celebrated and successful comic endings are also the most literally incredible. Our sense of rational probability clashes with our desperate need to live happily ever after in our fictional worlds, and the greatest comedies somehow find an ironic significance in the tension between these two different expectations. The classical critics, with their often literal-minded approach to poetic truth, observe but never quite pin down this dialectic of realism versus contrivance, decorum versus wish fulfillment. Bernardino Daniello, another Renaissance critic, in the course of one of those tedious lists of rules for the dramatist, gives an apparently unintentional illustration of my argument: "Comedy should not exceed the limit of five acts, nor comprise less . . . nor must any deity be brought in, except in cases where man is unable by his own efforts to unravel some tangle without divine aid and intercession."[15] There is a faint note of comic incongruity in such a passage, where one can see the classical conscience, caught in its own mutually exclusive critical principles about character and plot, trying to have it both ways. Deities are not appropriate among the "lowly and commonplace" events of the comic stage, but they may be a necessary last resort if neither the character nor the playwright can, "by his own efforts," bring the life and the work to perfection.

Thus the comic happy ending, contrived out of opposing approaches to reality, often evokes opposing interpretations and an ironic tension between them. Watching the fortunate resolution to which we always knew the characters were inevitably bound, the playwright may indeed invite us to feel what the classical critics demanded: that these feigned deeds "nevertheless could happen." But the playwright may also draw our attention to the ropes and pulleys of the deus ex machina and, indulging us with a beneficent vision of fate, may at the same time suggest "this is not the way it would happen." As the comic conception of character expresses an ambiguous cynicism, which either degrades or merely accepts the world as it "really" is, so the comic conception of plot expresses an ambiguous optimism. The happy ending magnifies the world with its infinite sense of the possible, and diminishes it with its ironic sense of the impossible. Consider, for example, how in several eccentric tragicomedies, Euripides deliberately changes the traditional accounts of his mythic heroes and heroines, allowing them to achieve the happy endings that the original stories and previous dramatic versions had alike denied

to them. Each of these hybrid plays disappoints the normal generic and narrative expectations of its audience, and then concludes with the same mysteriously ambiguous lines.

> Many are the forms of what is unknown.
> Much that the gods achieve is surprise.
> What we look for does not come to pass.
> God finds a way for what none foresaw.
> Such was the end of this story.[16]

Strangely enough, this apparent proverbial and poetic description
of our human reality also explicitly denies the possibility of knowing that reality. In one of the plays that so concludes, we are asked
to accept that the Trojan War was actually fought over a phantom
version of the title character, and that Helen and Menelaus were
finally reunited to escape together from the barbarian kingdom to
which coincidence had somehow brought them both. Such was
the end of *this* story. But in the telling of it, what we looked for did
not come to pass; it was Euripides himself who found a way for
what none foresaw. Do these final lines, which put the playwright
in the position of the gods, express a sincere evocation of the
mystery of our existence, or a savage irony about the limits of our
knowledge?

I shall have more to say about this most ingeniously perverse of
comic and tragicomic writers in the final section. For the moment,
what seems clear enough is that, as Aristotle suggests, audiences
wish to see their sympathies rewarded and will accordingly do
their best to believe in the happy ending under the right set of
theatrical circumstances. An audience demands that the figures on
the stage earn their own good fortune, not only or even necessarily
through their moral worth and endeavor as *characters*, but
through the intricacy and variety of their actions and words as
actors. A happy ending is thus a gift of art, and as art itself is both
a "mirror of nature" and a tangible performance bought and sold
like other commodities in a social setting, so the happy ending
reflects both what people are and what they want. Many of the
greatest playwrights have, in their particular resolutions of a plot,
deliberately emphasized the ironic gap between pleasing and portraying the world. The progression of Shakespeare's comedies, for

further example, reveals him gradually exploring that logical fallacy that he gave as title to one of his oddest comic plays: *All's Well That Ends Well*. I believe that Shakespeare never wholeheartedly accepts, and increasingly despairs of, the happy ending as an adequate representation of human reality. In *A Midsummer Night's Dream,* the playwright conveniently rearranges the four lovers with sympathetic, albeit implausible, magic, and the final scene portrays a ludicrous tragedy about the final separation to which these same lovers might very well have come. *As You Like It,* similarly, ends with an all too obviously contrived wedding of every available bride and groom, and a perfunctory disposal of what could have been serious impediments to the plot. By those puzzling late plays, which modern criticism calls "romances" but which retain the general plot structure (though not the unities) of Greek and Roman New Comedy, Shakespeare is still questioning if a happy ending can ever fully justify the perturbations that precede it. In *Cymbeline,* Jupiter tells the ancestors of long-suffering Posthumus,

> Who best I love, I cross; to make my gift,
> The more delay'd, delighted. Be content,
> Your low-laid son our godhead will uplift.
> (5.4.101–3)

This sounds more like a practicing playwright rationalizing the demands of dramatic construction than like a genuine deity explaining his strange and mysterious ways. Again the playwright stands in the place of the divine, since it is only he who can truly promise a fortunate conclusion. The ending of *A Winter's Tale* is Shakespeare's most drastic experiment with dramatic solutions and resolutions. When the queen's statue comes to life, we can accept neither the literal magic of this resurrection nor the "logical" explanation that Paulina had concealed Hermione for the full sixteen years. As Paulina puts it,

> That she is living,
> Were it but told you, should be hooted at
> Like an old tale; but it appears she lives.
> (5.3.115–17)

Forestalling conjecture and explanation alike by his importunate haste in terminating the play, Shakespeare here seems to tease the audience with its eagerness to accept what "appears" on the comic stage—where nothing, least of all this ending, is actually real. Our incredulity, as Shakespeare apparently understood, vanishes in the face of this wish-fulfilling denial of mortality, this reconciliation with the irrevocably lost.

Some later comedians have exploited the latent irony of all happy endings for more than art's sake alone. The ironic gap between the mirror and the performance, between realism and contrivance, takes on a darker significance, and raises questions that are realistic in a different sense. John Gay's *Beggar's Opera* may be the first comedy in the tradition that explicitly identifies the deus ex machina with the playwright, whose concrete embodiment on the stage produces a magical happy ending which the play's events had made literally impossible. The deciding factor in this play is not the gods, but the state. As the officers prepare to lead Macheath to his imminent and inevitable execution, the beggar-playwright of the title and one of his actors interrupt the play.

> PLAYER. But, honest Friend, I hope you don't intend that *Macheath* shall be really executed.
> BEGGAR. Most certainly, Sir—To make the piece perfect, I was for doing strict poetical Justice.—Macheath is to be hang'd; and for the other Personages of the Drama, the Audience must have suppos'd they were all either hang'd or transported.
> PLAYER. Why then, Friend, this is a down-right deep Tragedy. The catastrophe is manifestly wrong, for an Opera must end happily.
> (Scene 16, lines 1–10)[17]

The beggar, of course, is actually confused about that topic of contemporary literary debate to which he so confidently refers. His intended conclusion is the reverse of "poetic justice"—in other words, real, legal justice. Gay's audience knows perfectly well that Macheath must suffer for his crimes, and can indeed suppose that "the other Personages of the Drama" must be "either hang'd or transported." But as Aristotle suggested in his day, and as the Player agrees, "the taste of the town" is generally for plays that end happily. It is only on stage that we are reluctant to let charming and sympathetic characters go to the gallows. What the audience demands and gets is the reassuring, strictly inconsistent justice of the comic poet:

> BEGGAR. . . . in this kind of Drama, 'tis no matter how absurdly things are brought about. —So—you Rabble there—run and cry a Reprieve—let the Prisoner be brought back to his wives in triumph.

Even for us, living under at least a slightly more enlightened legal system, the *Beggar's Opera* still yields an uncomfortable sense that our deepest instincts, as manifest in our theatrical sympathy, run counter to our society and its regulations. In Brecht's version of the play, Macheath is reprieved even more implausibly by a messenger from the queen; and the final words of the play, enunciating Gay's unspoken irony, direct the actors to "sing the chorale of the poorest of the poor," because "in reality their end is generally bad."[18]

3   From Irony to Transcendence

To the critics who accompany the long history of comedy on the stage, the idea of comedy has truly been the slippery eel of W. C. Fields's simile, or the metaphoric servant of two masters that intrigued Freud. The critical issues raised by comedy refuse to remain discrete or consistent, and each attempt to define the sources and resources of laughter suggests an equal but opposed interpretation. The question of comedy's "realism," for example, intersects with the quite different question of social class in a thoroughly confusing and contradictory manner. As we have seen from a variety of angles, the classical critics found one source of comedy's verisimilitude in comedy's alleged "lowness." At the outset of our own century, Henri Bergson argued by contrast that "it is only in its lower aspect, in light comedy and farce, that comedy is in striking contrast to reality: the higher it rises, the more it approximates to life; in fact, there are scenes in real life so closely bordering on high-class comedy that the stage might adapt them without changing a single word."[1] This observation makes me think of an amusing situation reported in Pepys's diaries, when he is disturbed by some other spectators next to him at a fashionable play, only to realize that he finds their conversation more amusing than the dialogue on the stage.[2] (Pepys might have been so open to distraction because he was watching a heroic tragedy at the time.) On the other side of the dialogue of art and life, however, a practicing playwright like Congreve insists that "if a Poet should steal a discourse of any Length from the Extempore discourse of the two wittiest Men upon Earth, he would find the scene but coldly receiv'd by the Town."[3] And it was Congreve's own drama, a comedy of high verbal wit that mirrors the "follies" of men like Pepys and his upper-class contemporaries, that Lamb called "artificial." The bits of critical theory we have been considering seem to touch two poles of an apparent transformation in cultural attitudes. Plato thought it was degrading to play a part on stage or in life; good citizens, he enjoined, should leave acting to slaves. At the end of the seventeenth century, the theater remained a slightly suspect profession, but the vision of life as itself a play or performance began to take on a very different sense of elegance and charm. Somewhere over the centuries, a slavish humiliation becomes an elegant refinement, and the change sets its mark on comic theory.

In all its ages and forms, comedy continues to reflect and embody these paradoxes of life and art. We enjoy comic theater not despite, but because of its dialectical tension of conflicting visions and attitudes. Comedy allows us to see the face of reality with double vision: sometimes, like Gulliver in Brobdingnag, with its pores and blemishes grotesquely magnified; sometimes, as if in a fun-house mirror, with our companions and ourselves ambiguously distorted and yet familiar. We have found that comedy evokes certain oppositions of meaning and interpretation, and, strangely enough, these pairs match one another—not with that logical consistency that, in any case, has always been anathema to the comic spirit, but still with a revealing pattern of significance.

Life	Art
Mirror	Performance
Character	Plot
Realism	Fantasy; wish fulfillment
Cynicism	Optimism
Ideology	Utopia

This fearful symmetry is just an attempt to specify comedy's complex and two-faced approach to "reality," to understand why comedies far separated in time and space seem both consistently similar and unexpectedly new. The last pair of terms extends and clarifies the rest. Comedy conveys an ideological vision in its malice and intolerance, its prevailing sense of the corruption of human character—a vision that expresses the ruling assumptions, the convenient rationalizations, of a particular historical moment. In this aspect, comedy emphasizes the mode, the fashion, the here and now, indulging in the differences and distances between human beings, and embodying the "holiday humor" that is just an inverted reflection of the everyday. But to describe this aspect of comedy is also to suggest its opposite. Comedy says *these are the conditions that prevail,* but the saying raises a laugh that mocks those personified and prevailing conditions. A radical sense of human community, a reformer's zeal for equality, a leveler's vision of society without its distinctions—all these also emerge from comedy's cynical and simplistic declaration that "the world is all alike." Comedy is both fierce and forgiving: laughing the old vices out of countenance, but also preserving, against all odds, what one critic has aptly called "the people's unofficial truth."[4] A comic play may be adamantly ideological and seek to "vindicate and proclaim the ruling class" of its age and society, or, crystallizing a vision of timeless utopia, it may strive instead "to lay the plans for the future dwelling place of a new class."[5] The comic spirit locks us in familiar cages but at the same time holds out the promise of a threshold.

Even children learn the distinction between *laughing at* and *laughing with,* and it is not hard to see a kind of double face within the familiar twisted features of the comic spirit. The hard part is that both of comedy's visions or aspects can be found, held in dialectical tension and opposition, within a single play. Since the ideological and utopian sides of comedy finally represent two different kinds of moral purpose, we can understand why the question of comedy's effect on society and the human soul provokes the most striking divergences of critical opinion. Plato, as we have already seen, was deeply suspicious of the comedy he knew, but from a different historical perspective, his negative arguments stand as ironic praise of comedy's contagious and irrepressible power. "There is a principle within," Plato argues, "which is disposed to raise a laugh, and this was once kept in order by you because you were afraid of being thought a buffoon, but is now let loose again and encouraged by theatre, and you are often unconsciously betrayed into playing the comic poet in your own person" (*Republic* 10.606).[6] Stronger than the inhibitions of reason and social constraint, binding together the comedian and his audience, the comic spirit seems somehow to influence and reflect upon our sense of ourselves as members of a community. From Aristotle on, however, critics would suggest that art is insulated from the real workings of society, and that, accordingly, comedy's malice and satire, its uninhibited buffooneries and cynical appraisals of society, were purged away from the human soul in the very process of their expression. Aristotle's doctrine of *katharsis* was linked specifically to tragedy, but he probably also believed, as an anonymous Peripatetic commentator later deduced, that comedy purged "pleasure and laughter" from its audience as tragedy purged pity and fear.[7] Linked, by contrast, to Plato's idea that drama waters the passions, and with its overtones of a pre-scientific physiology, the idea of the dramatic catharsis remains a mysterious and unproven hypothesis. Most criticism of comedy, nevertheless, retains its basic implication: that comic plays are somehow different from what they seem and that they invite us to indulge in rebellious and cynical laughter only so that we may put those emotions away from our lives when the play is over.

In other words, the same kind of theater that had, for Plato, a genuinely subversive effect on the order and regulation of society, was, for Aristotle and most of his critical descendants, merely a therapeutic, temporary indulgence in disorder. "I am glad for a season," writes Lamb in ironic defense of comedy against the moralists, "to take an airing beyond the diocese of the strict conscience. . . . I come back to my cage and my restraint the fresher and more healthy for it."[8] Most contemporary criticism of comedy retains this Saturnalian accent, suggesting that comedy has the same oblique, inverted relation to reality that holidays have to the workaday world. The real purport of a comedy, in this kind of criticism, is exactly opposite from what it seems to express. Indulging us with festivity and celebration, comedies really try to lead us "back from a world of cakes and ale."[9] Here, for example, are three more attempts to prove that, for all its apparent rebelliousness, the genre remains essentially conservative of the social order:

> it is of the very essence of comedy that it should not express the code of the period, but that Saturnalian spirit of rebellion against the code, in those who nevertheless acknowledge it, which in all ages takes the form of wit and laughter.
> (Elmer Edgar Stoll)[10]

> Comedy, violating the stage convention, says, "Ah, but this is only a play; these characters are abnormal; or if the license of their abnormality is our secret desire and these sins our foibles, they are to be ritually expelled by our social laughter, and can secretly be enjoyed in real life with impunity." . . . Basically comedy is approval, not disapproval, of present society, it is conservative, not liberal. (Albert Cook)[11]

> People watch the fall of the ideal bird as it flies over the vapor of stagnant water and they laugh. . . .
>   Comedy is the literary genre of the conservative parties.
> (Ortega y Gasset)[12]

In their own contexts, in their own terms, all these arguments seem quite plausible. Together, they form a middle-of-the-road view of comedy that does not, however, entirely refute two other equally plausible arguments coming at it from different ends of the moral and ideological spectrum. The Saturnalian approach suggests that comedy is implicitly conservative, but conservative thinkers have themselves frequently argued, as Samuel Johnson did of Congreve, that the "ultimate effect" of comic plays was "to relax those obligations by which life ought to be regulated."[13] From Plato to Renaissance puritans like Stubbs and Gosson, to Jeremy Collier's immensely influential *Short View of the English Stage* (1698), a moral, religious, and conservative tradition of what George Meredith called *agelasts* (opponents of laughter), affirms and reaffirms a fundamental distrust of the comic impulse. Oddly enough, modern Marxist critics find one point of ironic agreement with this conservative tradition from which they depart in almost every other way. They too discover a genuine power in the comic spirit, even though they seek to extoll rather than inhibit that power. Accordingly, as the modern Russian critic Mikhail Bakhtin has convincingly argued, comedy expresses "the defeat . . . of all that oppresses and restricts"; it is an idiom "never used by violence and authority."[14]

No one who can remember the hideous laughter of Hitler and his storm troopers as recorded in *The Triumph of the Will* can agree with the Marxist vision of comedy's radical purity. But, then, no one who has vicariously triumphed over *The Great Dictator* along with the great comedian who chanced to resemble him can ever deny the ironic power that comedy places in the hands of the victims and underdogs. Laughter can quite conveniently be used by the voice of an authority against the outsiders who challenge it, and also by those outsiders against the restrictions of the powers that be. If some jokes express a united social viewpoint that mocks those who deviate from it, other jokes are, as Freud realized, "highly suitable for attacks on the great, the dignified, and the mighty, who are protected by internal inhibitions and external circumstances from direct disparagement."[15] Thinking back to the poles of comic contradiction, we can see that the Saturnalian view of comedy pits the *performance* against the *mirror*—that is, comedy is seen as *merely* art, which thus makes no real challenge to life. Conversely, both the moral suspicion of comedy and the sense of comedy as triumphantly revolutionary share an ultimate belief that comic drama portrays and also shapes the world, that its utopian vision can bring pressure to bear on the prevailing ideology.

I believe it is in the nature of comedy to evoke these opposed interpretations of meaning and purpose. After all, criticism is rational and, as Plato and Freud alike realized, reason is the fundamental target of comedy, the focus of its ingenious techniques of wit and humor. Perhaps this is why (at least until our own times, when critics desperately discover a merit worthy of analysis in all kinds of subgenres and forgotten texts), criticism has been so reluctant to grant comedy the literary status enthusiastically given to tragedy, epic, and narrative. Perhaps too, those

critics who affirm comedy's upside-down conservatism and defuse the explosive significance of the comic rebellion are merely
themselves part of the inevitable irony of the comic process—
which allows us to express emotions hidden even from ourselves,
and which cloaks its serious messages in ridiculous yet appealing
disguises. Those who look forward and those who look back,
revering what history can be or what it has been, seem to find
in comedy the same kind of menacing weapon or limitless tool.
Comedy, we can only conclude, goes both ways. As a modern
classicist argues, returning to the paradoxical doctrine of *katharsis*, the drama in general

> provides relief by giving free outlet to repressed emotion
> through such channels as the practice of confession or partici-
> pation in public festivals. . . . Therefore the arts are conserva-
> tive of the social order, in that they relieve the pressure on its
> members, but at the same time they are subversive, because they
> promote a recurrence of the stresses which they stimulate in
> order to relieve. They are a form of the organization of social
> energy, and the flood which they set in motion may, at any
> moment, in favorable conditions, reverse its direction.[16]

Or consider Freud's analysis of a joke that attacks the institution
of marriage: "A wife is like an umbrella—sooner or later one
takes a cab."[17] As Freud observes, "one does not venture to
declare aloud and openly that marriage is not an arrangement
calculated to satisfy a man's sexuality." Both despite and because
of this inhibition, "the strength of this joke lies in the fact that
. . .—in all sorts of roundabout ways—it *has* declared it." The
familiar piece of cynicism may ease our discomfort about marriage simply by expressing it; at the same time, it stands as an
ironic reminder that our institution does not answer to the deepest
facts of our being.

   In other words, our comedies represent and reflect our dupli-
ties, our intricate ways of naming ourselves. Human beings, like
their comedies, are also self-divided, torn by oppositions of meaning and interpretation—between corruption and virtue, between
the merely genteel and the truly noble, between a commitment to
personal advantage and an unselfish devotion to the greatest good

for the greatest number. These dilemmas of our social existence intersect the deeper paradox of life itself: we cannot live by bread alone, but we must have bread to live.

> Is there no saving means, no help religious
> For a distressed gentlewoman to live by?
> Has virtue no revenue?[18]

asks a character from one of Middleton's comedies. Comedy answers, cynically, in the negative; and then turns around and delivers the unexpected inheritance, as if to say: money can't buy happiness, but it sure helps; you preach that money is the root of all evil, but you also recognize its power "to command goods, enlist services, induce cupidity, promote avarice, invite to crime";[19] and you obey the imperatives of both visions. When a young man in Plautus asks a procurer for credit, and criticizes her lack of generosity, she answers simply: "Why blame me for doing my duty? No one has ever painted, sculpted or written about a madame like me being generous to a customer—if she wants to be prudent."[20] Or, as she might also have asked him, with the even deeper irony of a later comic writer,

> . . . where else, but on stages, do we see
> Truth pleasing, or rewarded honesty?[21]

A different young man in the same situation asks Ariosto's Lena for credit toward his object of desire, and promises "God be my witness." But his antagonist replies, "I've no use for a witness who can't be called into court."[22] The audience laughs, and then also remembers, in some back corner of mind and memory, that the laughter is finally directed at our whole human predicament, at this world bewilderingly split between the corporeal and the divine, the mundane and the transcendent. We look toward heaven, but we must also deal with the drainage; the philosopher enraptured by the stars will eventually fall in the ditch. Perhaps such certainties are the only wisdom: it is no laughing matter, but it is the source of the comic spirit.

In the following chapters of this essay, I will consider some specific examples of dramatic comedy, arranged under two basic headings. The selection is obviously neither comprehensive nor even representative, and nearly all the plays and playwrights, depending on one's specific point of view, are somewhat out of the ordinary. But then, it is not easy to find a truly "typical" comedy. The genre remains an unpredictable combination of ancient conventions and topical allusions, stock situations and outlandish novelty. In one sense, the Plautine farce is not unlike the television sitcom, and the same jokes, the same comic targets, the same notes of satire and cynicism, reverberate through the whole history of the genre from Aristophanes to this season's standup sensation. In another sense, all the best-loved comedies and comic stylists seem somehow unique, irreducible, inimitable. Even a generalizing critic like Northrop Frye sometimes finds himself admitting "*The Merchant of Venice* seems almost an exception," and "*Volpone* is exceptional."[23] On almost anyone's list of the most famous comedies of stage history are plays like the *Amphitryon, Le Misanthrope, The Way of the World,* and *The Importance of Being Earnest,* which have always been considered unusual or eccentric. In this book, I am arguing that a dialectical process goes into that peculiar vision, spirit, or pleasure we recognize as comic, and I have chosen plays that most clearly illustrate that dialectic in action. Insofar as these plays reveal extreme tendencies of the comic spirit, they reflect more clearly on the tradition from which they spring.

In the second section, I will be considering plays from the classical tradition in which comedy's opposing visions remain separately audible, jostling each other, and evoking an ironic tension. The demands of the "mirror" exert an ever-greater pressure on the conventions of "performance"; the cynical view of life personified by comedy's typical characters coexists uneasily with the optimism of comic plots. These comedies find their particular effects in an intrinsic and inevitable irony, for their happy endings are often the opposite of what one has any reason to expect, and they somehow both criticize and praise the world as it "really" is—and as they affirm it must be. Watching this kind of play, what you see is not necessarily what you get.

In certain magic moments of art and culture, however, ideology merges with utopia, and a genuine faith draws from humanity a belief in and a personal responsibility toward the future. Thus we get a few rare and precious plays like those we will consider in the third section, plays that portray history itself as a divine comedy before whose final reconciliation all humanity is indeed alike. These comedies indulge in irony and yet transcend it, express an extravagant cynicism which finally exhausts and transforms itself, and while denying that this has ever been the best of all possible worlds, seem confident that the comic spirit can point us in the direction of a better one. The happy ending of the theatrical performance holds out a larger, transcendent hope of grander happy endings, reconciling not only the characters but also the opposing visions of comedy. These special comic plays prove, once and for all, that laughing matters.

I have been arguing that the comic spirit faces the world with a constantly shifting perspective of mockery, derision, resignation, and praise. There are, finally, at least two different purposes within this cherished form of dramatic entertainment. The best definition I can find for them comes from a celebrated, though usually slightly misquoted piece of rhetoric. Nowadays, the lines I wish to borrow are often ascribed to Robert Kennedy, whose untimely assassination is one of those unhappy events that proves reality to be more tragic than tragedy. They actually come from George Bernard Shaw's *Back to Methusaleh,* where the serpent, that most subtle of all the creatures of the stage, complains that Adam and Eve merely ask questions about what *is,* instead of, like himself, imagining what might be.[24] The same terms, adapted to criticism, will serve to define the paradox of comedy. I conclude, to alter slightly the famous paraphrase of Shaw's serpentine distinction, that some comedies see things the way they are and ask *why,* but some comedies dream things that never were, and say *why not.*

Two

Comedy and Commerce:

An Ironic Partnership

4 The Plautine Success Story

—Okay, this is a stick-up, your money or your
life!
(*Long pause*)
—I'm thinking it over!
JACK BENNY, radio dialogue

Both before and after the great period of
what is usually called Comedy of Manners,
the comic spirit reveals our enduring interest in the intricacies and absurdities of
human society. The effect of the joke in this
chapter's epigraph stems partly from
theatrical convention and partly from our
own feelings about money and life. Our
laughter proclaims that *we* would not need
to "think it over." The joke fulfills our expectations of Jack Benny's miserliness (a
modern version of an ancient comic target) and humors our own
presumed sanity. Like both characters in this little dialogue, however, we are all more or less involved with getting and hanging on
to money, and the punch line does perversely affirm, as Shaw says
and we all implicitly acknowledge, that "money is the counter
that enables life to be distributed socially."[1] If the joke lets us
enjoy Benny's flirtation with death, it also invites us to ponder
that identity of money and life that is embodied by his momentary
confusion. Of course, Jack Benny the comedian also made a great
deal of money in the real world by pretending to be cheap. As we
shall see, comedy has always had both actual and thematic connections with the economic aspects of the theater.

In fact, critics throughout the centuries have suggested that comedy, like money, is a sort of social tool with which the community keeps misfits and eccentrics in their proper places. Portraying "the most ridiculous and scornful sort" of humanity, as Sir Philip Sidney phrases a familiar classical argument, comedy makes it "impossible that any beholder can be content to be such a one."[2] The idea would persist in later, more complex theories of the comic process. "Laughter," writes Henri Bergson at the outset of our own century, "is really and truly a kind of social 'ragging.' "[3] Having suggested an extraliterary approach to the subject by titling his essay *Le Rire*, Bergson proceeds to argue that comic drama is not finally a mode of artistic expression at all. Comedy "follows an impulse of social life," he concludes, and, therefore, "It is not *disinterested* as genuine art is." The emphasis is mine, and suggests the contrary direction that my argument will take. Comedy is not just society's tool to use on us; it can also be our tool to use in understanding society. Comedy's lack of detachment, its keen involvement in the affairs of the human community, represents its special power, not its fatal flaw. Showing us partly what we are and partly how we see ourselves, comedy is no more and no less disinterested than we are.

In fact, this word that looms so large in Bergson's drastic reduction of comedy contains, in its own background, the same paradoxes of meaning we will be finding in comedy itself. *Interest,* throughout what the Oxford English Dictionary frankly calls its "obscure" history, hovers between converging spiritual and concrete meanings. Its earliest uses in English (and French) largely retain the sense of the medieval Latin *interesse,* "to concern," referring to an objective or legal share in something. Subsequently, parallel branches of meaning run in two different yet oddly related directions. The word took on a general sense referring to personal advantage, while the familiar, specifically financial sense emerged as an ingenious rhetorical evasion. Then, as now, people took a keen interest in the fate of their money; this is obvious not only from the formal content of comic plays but also in the faintly comic manner with which our word transforms itself. In the Middle Ages, if one man borrowed from another, no fee could be charged him simply for the use of the money over a span of time—this would be *usury,* a very serious matter. But if the first man failed to return the money at the agreed time, the second man could charge him a fee for *damna et interesse*—what we call today "damages"—since it was obviously disadvantageous to be without the money longer than expected. In the sixteenth century, the church rescinded its prohibition of usury, and a capitalist society continued to grow from the payment and collection of what would still be called *interest*.

Meanwhile, an even longer interchange of nuance and metaphor extended the word from its original objective sense of having a share in something to an almost indefinable sense of intellectual fascination and concern. The original meaning, in its most general sense, we may now express as *self-interest*; and now we can be *interested* in something for subjective reasons of curiosity or spiritual attraction. In fact, we can find something *interesting* in this sense even when we are *disinterested* concerning it—that is, impartial, without pressing personal, legal, or financial needs in the matter. Critics, for example, are supposed to be disinterested, but I am doubtful whether artists can even pretend to the same detachment. What Bergson denied to the spirit of comedy is precisely this aesthetic distance, this dispassionate objectivity, that most modern criticism demands from art. But I have argued already that plays are both a reflection of social reality and a living part of that reality. In a simple and specific sense, writers of comedy have had about as much desire to make money in the living theater as they have had to fulfill any of the supposed moral or social functions of the drama. This fact may help explain the nature of plays, but it does not diminish their value. I am arguing that comedy is interesting because it emerges in the form and shapes of interest; because the great comedians' motives always reveal the same mixture of social pretense and genuine greed as those of the society they entertain and scorn.

Still, "it remains significant," as Raymond Williams argues, "that our most general word for attraction or involvement should have developed from a formal objective term in property and finance."[4] A similar conjunction of matter and spirit characterizes the history of comedy. Whatever ends comedy has served, whatever social or psychological functions it has fulfilled, it has always been of intrinsic economic worth. People take pleasure in the experience of comedy and will pay for that pleasure. At the same time, with fascinating illogic, people have tended to scorn the makers of comedy—almost as much as they have scorned the practitioners of that perhaps slightly older profession dealing with more tangible pleasures. This is a contradiction bound up with bourgeois values of thrift and acquisition. Comedy is lucrative for the comedians, but to middle-class society over a period of centuries, it seemed insultingly nonproductive. This trifle, this mere entertainment, not only makes its spectators pay to be idle, but even allows its makers to earn considerable amounts of money without really accomplishing anything.

The theater is obviously not the only intangible commodity in our history. But there has often been a special suspicion of the theater among some classes and commentators: partly a resentment that the performers make something out of nothing, and partly a sense of indignation that they seduce other people into wasteful enjoyment. Having laughed at the actors all day, writes Plato, you will find yourself with less self-control at home (*Republic* 10.606). The churches are empty, complains a Renaissance schoolmaster, but "Wyll not a fylthe playe, wyth the blast of a trumpette, call thyther a thousand?"[5] To a wide spectrum of Renaissance society, the players were drones sucking "the honey stored up by London's laborous citizens."[6] From any perspective, they were both entrepreneurs and bohemians, both merchants of entertainment and vagabonds without place or living. They made their way in bourgeois society, but not really on its own terms.

Consider, in parallel example, how Horace looks back on Roman literature and denounces one of the earliest and best comic writers in his culture for selling out. Horace's *Epistle to Augustus* is an elegant and ironic survey of Greek and Roman literature; the poem's centerpiece, however, is a nostalgic description of bourgeois life. "At Rome," Horace muses, "it was long a pleasure and habit to be up at dawn with open doors, to set forth the law for clients, to pay out to sound debtors money under bonds, to give ear to one's elders and to tell one's juniors how an estate might be increased and ruinous indulgence curbed" (*Epistles* 2.1.103–7).[7] With the full resources of his verse, Horace poeticizes the mechanisms of trade and exchange, in all their multifarious detail. Our literary heritage yields no more perfectly and characteristically ironic expression of the bourgeois ideal: this image of work as a pleasure and a habit; this image of the young sitting at their elders' feet and learning how to make money. But Horace goes on to describe how an age of poetasters follows the age of businessmen, how a passion for literature has complicated Roman values:

> The fickle public has changed its taste and is fired throughout with a scribbling craze. . . . Yet this craze, this mild madness, has its merits. How great these are now consider. Seldom is the poet's heart set on gain: verses he loves, this is his one passion. Money losses, runaway slaves, fires   he laughs at all. To cheat partner or youthful ward he never plans. (108–21)

The reference to runaway slaves may be cheating a bit, of course, since this was the type of event Romans were accustomed to laughing about in the theater. But in any case, Horace is suggesting that there is virtue both in having money and in being superior to it. This poem praises the dealers and lenders, but also the dedicated artists who care more for their vocation than for "gain." In other words, poets may not earn big salaries or build the economy, but at least they don't cheat their partners.

The poem's ironic tone suggests this is not to be taken too seriously. A few lines later, however, a major comic poet will fall victim to the implied contradiction in Horace's attitude. "See Plautus," Horace directs us; "he is eager to drop a coin into his pocket and, that done, he cares not whether his play fall or stand square on its feet" (170–76). Notice that Horace deduces a personal greediness in the playwright from the carelessness it produced in his plays: the argument runs toward, not from, biography. Horace probably knew no more about the hard facts of Plautus's life than we do. But Plautus would remain, partly on Horace's authority, an enduring example of shoddy dramatic craftsmanship, of the peculiar Roman sense of humor, and of an artist who pandered to the public taste. Several centuries later, Gilbert Norwood would similarly see in Plautus a "complete indifference to dramatic structure," which is ascribable, somehow, to an excessive concern with the personal, an impure sense of vocation. The plays are "deplorable," charged Norwood, when they are "strongly suffused by Plautus' own personality and *interests*."[8]

Notice how ancient and modern critic, classicist and neoclassicist, both demand what T. S. Eliot called an "escape from personality"[9] and attack Plautus from some point anterior to literature itself. In fact, from what little evidence we have of his life, we can conclude that Plautus probably did write plays out of interest in both senses. He was enormously popular with Roman audiences, and in this sense, from the playwright's point of view at least, there was nothing deplorable about his plays.[10] Still, comedy's very popularity, to the critical audience, is both a cause and effect of its aesthetic crudity. "What taste could you expect" asks Horace, "of an unlettered throng, just freed from toil, rustic mixed up with city folk, vulgar with nobly born?" (*Ars Poetica* 212–13). There is something about the mingling of social classes in the theater and audiences "freed from toil" that makes the poet and critic especially unhappy.

As far as we can tell, Plautus was probably neither a very good businessman nor a particularly dedicated poet—yet he became something of both. A passage well known to scholars from the *Attic Nights* of Aulus Gellius is a portrait of a self-made man of the theater:

> Now Varro and several others have recorded that the Saturio, the Addictus, and a third comedy, the name of which I do not now recall, were written by Plautus in a bakery, when, after losing in trade all the money which he had earned in employments connected with the stage, he had returned penniless to Rome, and to earn a livelihood had hired himself out to a baker, to turn a mill, of the kind which is called a "push-mill."[11]

Even if the lifetime that Gellius carelessly recounts is mere inference from the plays, it is still striking that Rome's critics identified Plautus, in effect, with one of his characters. Rome saw its greatest comic playwright as both petit bourgeois and hired slave, a bungler who, against all odds, gets the last laugh. And I still like to imagine the future playwright working behind the scenes *in operis artificum scaenicorum*, whatever that precisely means; losing his hard-earned money in some business scheme and then composing hit comedies while working at the same push-mill to which, in those comedies, angry masters always threaten to send their unflappable slaves.

Even if this account is literally true, we have no way of knowing how Plautus learned Greek, became familiar with Greek New Comedy, and figured out how to use its forms in an accessible Roman theater. Cleverly enough, Plautus seems to have learned a theatrical lesson from the metaphysical vision of his comic model. In an era when political constraints had reduced the pretensions of the Athenian stage, the late Greek comic playwrights developed, as if in counterpoint, a conservative vision of the inconsequence of human actions. They portrayed the struggles of life as much ado about nothing, an ironic dialogue between chance and choice. We invariably choose wrongly, the New Comedians seem to suggest, but then we chance upon what we would have chosen anyway. The new formal convention of a happy ending expresses a fatalistic sense that we are mere pawns in the hand of an ironically disinterested goddess of Fortune—who is really the playwright, moving the characters to their assigned, beneficent fates. In this drama, whatever is, is right. Apparent malice is revealed as misapprehension. A goddess with this name speaks the prologue to one of Menander's plays, and explains that the forthcoming events will show how "by help of God . . . evil, even as it comes to being, turns to good."[12] Later audiences watched different aspects of this thoroughly ambiguous optimism realized on other comic stages. For Plautus himself, this comic vision may have had a certain relevance to his own situation. If the account of his life is true, his could be considered the classic story of the big break, and the forms of an alien and anachronistic comedy moved him from the push-mill to the comfortable stage. Here is comedy as a social tool in the reverse of Bergson's sense. To the playwright, this would scarcely have been much ado about nothing; it might have seemed, indeed, a case of all's well that ends well.

Certainly the theatrical self-consciousness that pervades Plautus's plays might well have been the product of this comedy of loss and restoration that Romans at least imagined him to have lived.

By the fourth century, Donatus was already complaining that Plautus *facit actorem uelet extra comoediam loqui* (makes the actors speak as it were outside of the play).[13] To modern readers, the authorial voice of the play seems to convey an even more strikingly mixed message. The various speakers of the prologues and epilogues approach the audience sometimes as preachers and sometimes as panders, their frankness collapsing the distance between artist and audience. At the outset of the *Amphitryon*, for example, the figure that steps on stage embodies a theatrical paradox. It is a human actor dressed, presumably, in the conventional costume of a slave, who speaks in the admonitory aspect of a god, and who then reminds the audience of the very things it would probably prefer to forget, the workaday complications left behind for the two hour's traffic of the stage:

> As all you gathered here would have me prosper you and bring you good luck in your buyings and your selling, yes, and advance you in everything; and as you would have me give a happy ending to your business affairs and speculations both at home and abroad, and crown your present and future enterprises with ample profit forever . . . as all of you want me to bless you in these things, in such degree will you—keep still while we are acting this play, and be fair and square judges of the performance.[14]

As you would profit in the world, advises Mercury the god of commerce, give your attention to this unprofitable play. This piece of illogic is the first joke of the comedy, and we confirm its ironic point by appreciating it. The abrupt shift in tone at the end of the passage is itself an attention-grabbing device in the manner of all entertainers "working a crowd." When Mercury next promises to summarize "the argument of this . . . *tragedy*," he also reacts to what may have been a real murmur of disappointment:

> What? Furrowing your brow because I announced a tragedy? I'm a god: I'll change it. I'll convert the play from tragedy to comedy, if you want it that way. I'll mix things up: let it be a tragicomedy! (Lines 52–59)

Here too, the joke conveys both flattery and ridicule of the audience. Centuries later, critics managed to underline Plautus's irony by placing his portmanteau word "tragicomedy"—chosen for its convolution of sound and meaning—at the center of a scholarly debate about the meaning of this hybrid genre.[15] In criticism as in life, there's many a true word spoken in jest. The expanded version of Plautus's joke that stretches through critical history is one more example of comic paradox, balancing comedy's official inconsequence against its obvious and enduring power.

Plautus apparently drew a theatrical lesson from the paradoxical vision of life in New Comedy. Instead of assuring the audience that a man will get what he wants despite his own best effort to defeat himself, Plautus assures the audience only that it will get as much entertainment as it paid for, despite the playwright's best efforts to defeat coherence. Both ancient and modern critics have noticed Plautus's realistic tone and general carelessness of dramaturgy—as compared, for example, with his contemporary Terence. Plautus's endings are less tidy, his *sententiae* more cynical. The optimism inherent in the convention of a happy ending rings slightly hollow. Often, Plautus qualifies the happiness of his endings by a simple refusal to emphasize the lines and resolutions of his own plots. At the same time, he was dramatist enough to exploit the inevitable tension between the borrowed conventions of comic optimism and his own realistic vision of a society where what is, many times, is wrong. At the end of the *Casina*, the lecherous husband is discovered and his designs frustrated, but the really crucial aspect of the happy ending—the revelation that Casina is actually the neighbor's daughter—is revealed as an afterthought in the epilogue. And the wronged wife agrees to forgive her husband for frankly theatrical reasons, because she doesn't want "to make this long play even longer" (1006). This is a "realism" that defies the usual requirements of realistic drama. Plautus did not discover this particular comic technique, which he could have seen in Aristophanes and probably in other lost Greek comedies. But Plautus has a special way of using this joke. Sometimes, he flatters the audience—as once, when one character refuses to explain the plot to another character because, as he puts it, the audience already understands it and the play is being acted for its benefit. Sometimes, however, Plautus expresses a disdain for the consumers of his art that points all the way forward to Shakespeare and Shaw. In the *Casina,* for example, Plautus holds up the happy ending as a mere convention to be duly observed, and then, asking the audience on behalf of the actors to "reward us with your applause," the playwright promises "Whoever does so shall always deceive his wife and have the mistress he desires." Here is the entertainer as pander, almost literally. Plautus seems instinctively to have understood the psychic roots of comedy's refined or unrefined pleasures.

Plautus's apparent carelessness, then, may conceal or express an awareness of the ironic relationship between comedy and society. Like one of his slave characters, Plautus *libertatem malitia invenit sua,* won his liberty by his craft. The victory seems to have left him with a powerful sense of how money mediates between the material and spiritual aspects of human life just as it does between author, actor, and audience on the stage. The basic plot of a Plautine comedy, usually involving a sum of money that must be paid for the young woman beloved by the *jeune premier,* embodies the paradox of the price versus the prize; the assumed existence of prostitution makes possible a crude but clear expression of money's connection to the pleasure principle. Money stands for the power of society's regulations (the father), even as it sums up the sources and resources of life. In the *Pot of Gold,* the miser Euclio goes to the market to buy food for his daughter's wedding banquet. "I go to the market and ask for fish," he explains, "It was very expensive! The lamb was expensive, the beef was expensive, the veal and chicken and pork—it was all expensive!" (372–74). So Euclio buys nothing, explaining "that's how I circumvented the whole crooked bunch of them." The audience laughs in recognition of the paradoxical nature of money, which has value only when exchanged for something else. Comedy has found miserliness an enduring target because it is an obsession that destroys its object; a need to possess the actual mineral stuff of wealth that denies the possessor the benefits and pleasures that wealth represents. The miser confuses the symbol with the actuality, the frustration with the fulfillment. In this play, more specifically, he confuses his ducats and his daughter. It happens that Euclio's grandchild is born at the same time his money is stolen, giving rise to one of the most famous scenes of mutual misapprehension in the history of comedy—when Lynconides confesses to Euclio his theft, not of the gold, but of the girl. Both Molière and Fielding would later try their hand at this same scene of *qui pro quo*, whose comic point, we may conclude, expresses an enduring sense of discomfort about the relationship of money and life.

Of course, in a typical Plautine play, the money that someone always needs to buy something particularly desirable is never "earned," but merely acquired by the "wit" of the trickster slaves. Perhaps Plautus, who also made his money through his wit, focused on a trickster figure partly because he was one too. Plautus's memorable slaves have been studied from every conceivable angle, from the anthropological to the linguistic, but they also embody and express familiar ambivalent feelings about money. A slave, after all, embodies the identity of money and life. And these articulate and irrepressible theatrical favorites, in their flights of rhetorical fancy, taunt the audience with fantasies of easy money, of getting something for nothing. "I'll be a poet," says Pseudolus in the play of the same name, "I'll create two thousand dollars that don't even exist yet" (*Pseudolus* 541). A different slave, having tricked a considerable sum of money out of his gullible master, exults "I don't think there is a single field in all Attica as fertile as this Periphanes of ours" (*Epidicus* 306–7). Transplanted to the fields of Italy or England, translated to the dialects of Machiavelli or Jonson, this perverse comparison between human credulity and biological fertility continues to indulge us with images of effortless, unearned wealth. The bourgeois Roman businessmen at whom Horace looks with nostalgia must have found the image especially appealing, despite, or because, it secretly gives the lie to their public values.

There is, of course, another way to look at it. Since the same spectators who laughed at Plautus's theatrical slaves were also slave owners in real life, one can argue that an insolent and fearless Pseudolus, an outrageously impudent Epidicus, were enjoyable for Roman audiences precisely because they were so obviously unreal. Certainly the slaves flirt with death and torture in a manner wholly implausible for living men—and, as Bergson put it, "we laugh every time a person gives us the impression of being a thing."[16] But Bergson's laughter, a triumphant expression of the *élan vital,* finds its characteristic targets in the misers and malcontents, in ludicrous fanaticism and paralyzing obsession. The Plautine slave conveys, instead, a Protean image of infinite flexibility; and we laugh as a person whom society has declared to be a thing reveals, instead, an unshakable vitality. It is true enough, as Paul Dunkin puts it, that "people do not pay to be reformed."[17] Plautus could not speak the real truth about his society any more than he could depict the real workings of fate. But at least his plays do not let a society of slave owners take complacent pleasure in their smooth-functioning system. The mischief of the tricksters, like the theatrical technique of the playwright, embodies and expresses the hidden comedy of a system much simpler than the creatures it tries to control.

One of Plautus's lesser-known plays will provide some final examples of his method. "The emptiest cinema-story ever exhibited," writes Gilbert Norwood, Plautus's most merciless modern critic, "has a Sophoclean subtlety about it if compared to the *Asinaria.*"[18] There is indeed something perfunctory about the way Plautus handles the traditional plot in this absurd little play, this Comedy of Asses. Even its first scene conveys the self-mocking tone and the quality of make-believe that pervade the work. As it begins, a slave is begging his master not to punish him, while making gruesome puns about specific Roman techniques of torture. Then the same master immediately enlists the slave's aid in a piece of comic mischief. It is almost a parody of the conventional situation. In this play, the *jeune premier* needs money to buy his mistress, as usual; but his unusual father wants him to have it. The only problem is that their respective mother and wife is less understanding; so the father commissions the slaves Libanus and Leonides to steal the money. The slaves conceive and execute an elaborate plot to defraud a trader of the payment for a pair of asses, owed to the household. But it turns out that the trader hands over the money only when the master gives his permission in person anyway, so the slaves' trickery has little real purpose or effect. Then, after they have gotten the money, the two slaves tease the young lovers in a long dancelike scene that is as theatrically effective as it is dramatically irrelevant. We witness in this play merely the greatest possible ado about nothing. Defeating suspense, drawing his plot out on the slightest of pretexts, the playwright pulls off the play with only minimal concessions to character and plot.

To a modern reader, however, there is a certain sense, behind the laughter, that all is not sweet, all is not sound. The prevailing tone of easy indulgence actually underlines the brutal cynicism of the play's humor, which enforces a growing association between life, love, language—and money. From its first lines, the humor of the play is shadowed with images of death. "If you lie to me today," Libanus warns his master, "may your wife outlast you by many years, and you die a living death with her alive" (20–23). The Saturnalian situation where the slave threatens the master is overlaid with a different and deeper cynicism. Libanus has threatened his master only with the simple reality of the master's life, a threat that expresses at once both the slave's impotence in any sphere beyond the rhetorical, and the comic wisdom that there are many different kinds of slaves. Later on, the audience learns how Argyrippus, like most of the conventionalized young men in Plautine comedy, is lovesick unto death. The young man complains *"nisi illud perdo argentum, pereundum est mihi"* (either that money goes to pot, or else my life must). Paul Nixon's translation captures some of the subtlety of Plautus's near pun, which gathers together the multiple ambiguities we have been considering. For one thing, the joke conveys a further sense of the sheer inconsequence of the play's events, since Argyrippus's salvation lies in a salable object for which, as we already know, money will be forthcoming. At the same time, the joke also embodies the relativity of money itself—which, in the play as in the world, must be both lost and gained, both spent and earned. The money simply leaves the young man's pockets and goes to somebody else's Pot of Gold.

In this case, the person gaining and (in some sense) earning the money is Cleareta, the mother and owner of Argyrippus's beloved. She steals the stage for one scene and remains a strangely sympathetic blocking character. Cleareta is neither the harlot-with-a-heart-of-gold whom Menander may have introduced into Western culture, nor the brutal procurer we find in other Plautine comedies. She has escaped from a life of destitution by trading on the favors of her daughter Philaenium. "Before I courted that girl of yours," Argyrippus taunts her, "you used to regale yourself on coarse bread in rags and poverty; yes, and gave hearty thanks to Heaven, if you got your bread and rags" (141–43). The real poverty and misery is kept off stage, but it has apparently produced in Cleareta that tone of comic cynicism that remains familiar to us through the ages. Her cool irony reminds both Argyrippus and the audience that, in a world governed by money, both lust and avarice have the same social shape:

> CLEARETA. You can always be sure of having her—if you pay the most.
> ARGYRIPPUS. When will the paying be enough? You're never satisfied!
> CLEARETA. And when will the having her, the loving, be enough? Are you never satisfied?
> (166–69)

To Argyrippus's complaints she interposes an ironic understanding of real life in a commercial society, a cynicism that reminds me of Brecht or Shaw. "When we go to the baker for bread, to the vintner for wine," she calmly explains, "we pay our money and get the goods. It's the same system here" (201–3). Whatever your other emotions, for a moment you must consider her, as she considers herself, simply a merchant offering *opera pro pecunia*, services rendered for cash. The happy ending, such as it is, will be sold and delivered with two willing partners to the transaction. And Cleareta herself takes on a theatrical solidity as she outfaces the young bourgeois who finds himself an unwilling miser at the table of love. This, as she reminds us, is simply the way of the world.

Plautus's method, in other words, is founded in a certain duplicity. The playwright's mood is both complacent and indignant; he conveys an indulgent sense of holiday and a cynicism of everyday life. Only by exploiting the tension between these two could

Plautus express what we have imagined to be "himself." Only by investing the theatrical presentation with an ironic self-consciousness that forces the spectators to see themselves as such, could he communicate what Dunkin finds in his work, "the reaction of a vigorous poor man to an oppressive capitalistic system."[19] If, as criticism, this judgment slightly overstates the case, it still shapes my own view of Plautus's savagely trivial plays. He was a playwright who let us have it both ways. He shows us a world where a ruling class can buy, sell, torture, and kill a slave class, in plays that dramatize, as Erich Segal put it, "the victimization of the ruling class by the lowly slave." This persuasive modern critic (who would gain considerable personal experience with the dynamics of popular entertainment) interprets Plautus's constant references to torture in the same Saturnalian terms that inform his general approach to Plautine comedy. According to Segal, the Roman spectators took a "special pleasure" in watching the slave go unpunished for the insolence and mischief that could realistically have earned him (in Segal's own colorful translation)

> hot-iron tortures, crucifixion, chains,
> Strappadoes, fetters, dungeons, locking, stocking,
>   manacles. . . . (548–49)[20]

It is true that, on stage, these torments are only threatened, never inflicted. But on which should we focus, the gibbet or the reprieve?

Plautus's purpose goes deeper, I believe, than a momentary, deliberate confusion of the punisher and the punished. Torture and pain, as the slaves' wit affirms, are the only wages of slavery, the final testimony to the tragic power of matter (money) over spirit (life). As Libanus tells Leonides, in a bitter version of the inheritance motif, torture is *testamento servitus legat tibi* (what you are down for in slavery's will). For some spectators, then and now, the slaves may be little more than comic gladiators, wielding and suffering the implements of power. But I think modern audiences, at least, can find in these passages the same "fine and elevating" qualities that Freud discovered in what he called "gallows humor." This is a type of wit made at no one's expense but one's own, a sort of gratuitous and desperate joke said when there is nothing else to say (as if a victim at the gallows, told it is Monday, should observe that his week was beginning well). These liberating, self-motivated, self-fulfilling instances of the comic spirit are, in Freud's analysis, an expression of "the ego's victorious assertion of its own invulnerability. It refuses . . . to be compelled to suffer."[21] The Romans were undoubtedly less squeamish about blood than we are, but their greatest comic playwright recorded the atrocities that pervaded his society (and ours), even as he minimized their horror by banishing their actual presence from his stage. In Plautus's happy endings, the interested self is rewarded, and the designing slave earns his freedom or at least escapes unpunished. Plautus is careful finally to let us off the hook, to defuse the threat of too much reality. But he never quite lets us forget, as he could hardly himself have forgotten, that the true stakes of the comic conflict are different from what they appear:

> LEONIDES. Hey, Libanus, a lover really suffers, doesn't he?
> LIBANUS. No way! Someone hung up by the heels suffers much
>   more, believe me!
> LEONIDES. I know it—I've tried it.
> (615–17)

5   Machiavellian Humor

Now we can acquit Plautus of an alleged offense which Gilbert Norwood thought put him "outside the pale of art, almost of civilization." This was "his practice of tying together—not only in the same play, sometimes in the same scene—modes of feeling and treatment utterly incongruous."[1] (Something about the drama in general and comedy in particular produces in critics the most peculiarly melodramatic posturings.) I am arguing that comedy, as genre, spirit, or experience, is specifically about the clash of incongruous modes of thought and feeling. Mikhail Bakhtin, similarly, defines what he calls "Renaissance realism" as just this sort of conflict or dialectic:

> Two types of imagery reflecting the conception of the world here meet at crossroads; one of them ascends to the folk culture of humor, while the other is the bourgeois conception of the completed atomized being. The conflict of these two contradictory trends . . . is typical of Renaissance realism. The ever-growing, inexhaustible, ever-laughing principle which uncrowns and renews is combined with its opposite: the petty, inert "material principle" of class society.[2]

Thus the gallows humor of the Plautine slave, the triumphant revolt of the ego against the fear and violence of political authority, is circumscribed by the Saturnalian conviction that, in real life, these are the conditions that prevail.

All of these are features of that hidden "seriousness" in comedy, that dark underside of the comic experience to which the occasional proverb, at least, testifies our awareness. The idea of "laughing to keep from crying," for example, has remained an enduring conceit in our culture. "If sometimes I laugh or sing," writes Niccolò Machiavelli in a letter dated April 16, 1513, "I do it because I have just this one way for expressing my anxious sorrow."[3] He has slightly misquoted the poet Petrarch, who had originally written of laughter "concealing" his sorrow. Appropriately enough, the line makes sense either way. But the small change does suggest a certain insight into the comic method of this great historian, political thinker, and occasional playwright. Like Plautus, Machiavelli was a man who turned to the comic drama only after failing in other kinds of endeavor. For the fifteen years preceding this letter, he had had an active career in Florentine politics, and the "sorrow" of which he speaks was that of his disgrace following the fall of the Florentine republic he had faithfully served. In the period of his retirement, Machiavelli produced not only the masterpieces of political theory and history on which his major reputation depends, but also what is conceded to be the finest Italian comedy of the Renaissance.

Machiavelli's life and work both reveal his use of comedy to express the most serious of things. After being unjustly implicated in a plot against the new Florentine state, Machiavelli was confined for a time in the dungeons of the Signoria, where he tasted some of the same ingenious devices of punishment and persuasion to which Plautus so vividly refers. In the two comic sonnets he composes in prison and addresses to Giuliano de'Medici, he is reminiscent of Plautus's peculiar strain of gallows humor. The lice are fat as butterflies, he writes, and the walls echo with the shrieks of tortured men;[4] it is no wonder he is distracting his mind with comic ironies. The sonnets may also have amused Giuliano to good purpose. After his release, Machiavelli retires to his farm at

San'Andrea and spends his time thinking and catching thrushes. In a letter to his friend Vettori, he depicts himself carrying a pile of cages on his back and resembling, interestingly enough, a Plautine slave—specifically "Geta returning from the port with Amphitryon's books." His own tragedy of misapprehension, his own comedy of social reversal, may have brought with them a special insight into theatrical convention. As his biographer reminds us, laughter was for Machiavelli both a weapon and a defense, a sort of pose or mask whose features, to paraphrase Aristotle, were ugly and distorted, disguising pain.[5]

There is some controversy over the date of composition and the biographical background of Machiavelli's *Commedia di Callimaco e di Lucretia,* better known as *Mandragola.* It is clear, however, from the prologue that the play was composed after the end of Machiavelli's active political career, and that he sensed a connection between the injustice that had been done to him and his new vocation as comic playwright. In fact, Machiavelli suggests in the prologue that he is writing drama out of *interest* in two senses:

> If this material—since really it is slight—does not befit a man who likes to seem wise and dignified, make this excuse for him, that he is striving with these trifling thoughts to make his wretched life more pleasant, for otherwise he doesn't know where to turn his face, since he has been cut off from showing other powers with other deeds, there being no pay for his labors.

He has known the patron and the jail, and now he turns to the comedian's undignified profession out of a sense of personal and public injury. Most scholars agree that *Mandragola* was written between 1513 and 1520, and Machiavelli's letters from this period make clear that the financial necessity announced in the prologue was no mere theatrical pose. "My condition is impossible," he writes in a letter to Vettori in April 1514.[6] A few months later, he is even more specific:

> It is impossible that I can remain long in this way because I am using up my money, and if God does not show himself more

favorable to me, I see that I shall be one day forced to leave home, and hire out as a tutor or a secretary to a constable, since I can do nothing else, or fix myself in some desert land to teach reading to boys, leaving my family here.[7]

At one point, in the words of his biographer, the former statesman accepts a commission "to go as ambassador, not of the republic to other republics and princes, but from one merchant to another." In this role, he travels to Genoa to supervise the settling of a case of bankruptcy, "and all he will now talk of is debts and credits; dye-stuff and cloth."[8] We merely note, in passing, that Machiavelli was another comic playwright who had observed capitalism from both within and without the privileged position of prosperity and rank.

His critics disagree about Machiavelli's intention and achievement in *Mandragola*. Some suggest the play has an essentially serious message, while others deny it contains "moral purpose" at all.[9] Sydney Anglo takes a middle position: "The *Mandragola*, in so far as it may be read as a serious comment on anything, seems to suggest that everybody is looking for personal gain, be it lust or loot."[10] Machiavelli does express, on many levels, the familiar comic cynicism, and he does explore the conflict and connection between desire and wealth, between real and financial value. In fact, like Plautus before him, Machiavelli speaks to us from the autobiographical prologue both as pander and preacher, asserting his mastery of the medium along with his scorn for the project. Even the opening line is double-edged: "God bless you, well-wishing hearers, since it appears that these good wishes depend on our pleasing you." This single sentence moves author and audience from a state of community to a complex and wary relationship of reciprocal self-interest. It is exactly the conflict between these two ways of looking at life that the play will examine, and the prologue holds up the theatrical situation as a prototype of society. Moreover, Machiavelli has a personal connection to the ambiguity of comedy's social position: comedy is "slight" and "trifling," but there is no pay for being "wise and dignified." At least he is confident in his ability to please the audience. He announces that "the author is not very famous, yet if you do not laugh he will be ready to pay for your wine." This money-back guarantee is another version of the association between comedy and intoxication which runs from Dionysus to W. C. Fields, and which here reduces the theater to a soporific commodity. Machiavelli reminds the audience "that the author, too, knows how to find fault, and that it was his earliest art; and in no part of the world where *si* is heard does he stand in awe of anybody, even though he plays the servant to such as can wear a better cloak than he can." The playwright is willing to play the theatrical pander, but also lets us know he's only in it for the money. The confusing alternation of seduction and satire in the prologue forms an apt introduction to a play that both attacks society and capitulates to it; that both concedes and questions the nature of money as a formal equivalent to life.

The prologue in effect sets up between author and audience the same relations that prevail among the characters on the stage, an uneasy but workable compound of flattery and prevarication. Nearly everyone in this play seems, like its author, to be looking out for his or her own self-interest in a world where merit has no guarantee of success and virtue no revenue. The characters and the plot alike suggest different aspects of the power of money over people. The parasite Ligurio, prime mover of the play's events, is a formal "marriage-broker" who will negotiate a different kind of human relationship for the same financial recompense. Messer Nicia, the play's comic butt, desperately wishes to have children, "being very rich" (the simple phrase in apposition is suggestive). Callimaco spends his money freely to satisfy his lust for Lucretia. The church is induced to bring its authority to assist the seduction, as Ligurio explains to Callimaco, by "you, I," and "money" (2.6). In this celebrated line, the parasite expresses, with the greatest possible concision, how money mediates between lives. The situation is more complicated than in Plautus, for in this play there is no simple price for the object of desire. Lucretia and her mother alike are said to be impervious to bribery; Nicia is not really miserly, only shallow; even Ligurio claims to be performing his part not only for profit, but also out of a "natural affinity" with

Callimaco. In many comedies, as in Plautus's, the emphasis is on what we cannot have and hold *without* money. Here, Machiavelli conveys a positive sense of what money *does:* how it can work behind the scenes of daily life in strange and mysterious ways; how it can buy what is not even for sale.

Machiavelli's characters act out a tightly constructed and single-mindedly efficient plot, in two senses of the word. "No comedy," asserts a modern critic, "accomplishes so much in so little space."[11] Here is what happens: Callimaco goes to Nicia disguised as a doctor and prescribes a potion of mandrake root as a cure for Lucretia's barrenness. He convinces Nicia that the potion will allow his wife to get pregnant, but that it will also kill the first man to sleep with her afterwards. Callimaco helps Nicia find someone else to sleep with Lucretia the first time, and finally contrives to be that someone else. In other words, as Machiavelli himself puts it in the prologue, the play depicts how a smart young fellow "greatly loved a prudent young woman and tricked her." But the author cannot resist adding, "I hope you'll be tricked as she was." So there are two kinds of conquest going on here. Callimaco's elaborate scheme has the same clockwork regularity, the same unities of time, place, and action, as Machiavelli's design for the whole play,[12] and both plots apparently demonstrate that everyone has his or her price. Callimaco succeeds in his sexual conquest of Lucretia, contriving to do so with her mother's approval, with the sanction of her church, and, finally, with the ultimate social confirmation of the audience's applause.

But the play also forces us to take some account of the figure who is the target of both Callimaco's scheme and Machiavelli's apparent cynicism. For Lucretia herself is distinct from the other infinitely accessible and infinitely desirable heroines who serve as the focus of desire, and of the plot, in so many other comedies. Her presence moves the play away from the traditional comic conflict between chance and choice, to an even more deeply ironic struggle between expedience and morality. Choice, rather than chance, is the prime mover of this play. Not every character understands the full situation of which he or she forms a part; but each, with the significant exception of Lucretia, freely and know-

ingly chooses to depart from the accepted moral code. Machiavelli gives us a gallery of amiable cynics who show a familiar
readiness to bend moral rules for their personal advantage. For
Sostrata, social realities and pressures are more persuasive than
the moral or religious sanctity of marriage, and she reminds her
daughter that "a woman who doesn't have any children doesn't
have any home" (3.11). Sostrata has been what the others call
a "lively" woman in her day, and she apparently views marriage
and children as necessary but unpleasant social constraints on her
sex, so that "when she got the idea that her daughter could have
this pleasant night without sin, she didn't stop begging, ordering,
encouraging Lucretia until . . . she consented" (4.2). Different
versions of Sostrata's attitude pervade the play. "I believe,"
Ligurio tells the Frate, lapsing into ironic sincerity within a passage of prevarication, "that good is what does good to the largest
number, and with which the larger number are pleased." "So be
it, in God's name," replies the Frate, "Do what you want to, and
let it all be done for God and charity" (3.4). In this exchange, the
savage irony contradicts but cannot extinguish the powerful sense
of fulfilled desire, the image of doing what one wants to do; and
a modern reader, at least, feels somehow pleased with both the
fulfillment and the irony. Machiavelli's dialogue reenacts its own
utilitarian philosophy: we are part of that "largest number"
whose pleasure defines our morality. The audience, in their growing involvement with the fast-moving and ingenious piece of mischief transpiring before them, must admit their complicity in it.

   For Lucretia herself, however, the only thing at issue is that she
must sleep with a stranger and that he must die in consequence. As
the moral forces of her world close in around her, with their
rationalizations of relative value and immediate utility, Lucretia
expresses the absolutism of her moral perspective with the same
concision we have seen throughout. "If I were the only woman left
in the world," she insists, "and the human race had to begin again
from me, I can't believe that such a way to do it would be per-
mitted to me" (3.10). Focusing on the one situation where presumably anyone would choose the expedient course, Lucretia
impresses us with her simultaneous and contradictory sense of in-

nocence and acquiescence. Hers is a moral view too simple for
social life, in which there are no distinctions between public and
private truth, one in which moral value transcends all conditions,
transcends life itself.

Of course, the opposing viewpoint prevails. But by stating the
conflict of the play in this way, we move toward a further sense of
how the poles of comic contradiction operate ironically upon one
another. In this play, the conflict between morality and expedience stands, as we have observed, in the place of the older comic
conflict between chance and choice; but then the victory of expedience is also a victory of choice. In other words, the play's
comic structure embodies the ideology of self-interest: Machiavelli suggests that the freer we are to choose, the less likely we are
to act according to the nominal moral code. Still, the events of this
play at least represent much ado about something. New Comedy
portrayed characters "struggling unawares against imminent
good fortune,"[13] at once denying the real consequence of human
choice yet still rewarding the interested self. In contrast, Machiavelli portrays characters who work knowingly and effectively for
their own self-interest and who make their own happy ending,
such as it is. Machiavelli's play was a new step in the evolution of
the comic spirit. New Comedy's politely optimistic vision depicts
how people could solve their personal, private, and familial prob-
lems with the fortuitous assistance of chance. Later, Plautus qualifies this already-ambiguous optimism with an alien, realistic tone
and an outsider's ironic skepticism. But in *Mandragola*, going one
step further, Machiavelli seems to have made a comedy of pure
"realism," pure cynicism.[14] Here is a social world where everyone
is out for him- or herself, so that, in a later poet's words,

> . . . if you think it fair
> Amongst known Cheats, to play upon the square,
> You'le be undone.[15]

Just so is Lucretia undone. In the actual resolution of the play,
however, Machiavelli leaves us with what I can only awkwardly
call a cynical optimism. Menander had spoken centuries earlier of
how his comedy would show how evil turns to good, and here, in

Callimaco's account of the play's sexual denouement, we see how
Lucretia herself turns the victory of expediency back into a new
kind of absolutism:

> I was anxious until three o'clock, and though I was having a
> very good time, it didn't seem to me right. But then I made my-
> self known to her and made her understand my love for her, and
> how easily, because her husband is so stupid, we could live in
> happiness without any scandal, and promised her that when
> God removed him, I'd take her as my wife. Besides my sound
> reasons, too, she felt what a difference there is between the way
> I lie with her and the way Nicia does, and between the kisses of
> a young lover and those of an old husband. After some sighs she
> said: "Your cleverness, my husband's stupidity, my mother's
> folly, and my confessor's rascality have brought me to do what
> I never would have done of myself. So I'm forced to judge that it
> comes from Heaven's wish that has ordered it so, and I'm not
> strong enough to refuse what Heaven wills me to accept. I take
> you then for lord, master, guide; you are my father, you are my
> depender; I want you as my chief good, and what my husband
> has asked for one night, I intend him to have always." (5.4)

There is a characteristic doubleness about this passage: we see
Lucretia making religious rationalizations for her own desire or,
perhaps, merely responding to this new "immoral" relationship
with the same commitment she had given to the morality whose
agents have so thoroughly betrayed her. The schematic, fairy-tale
sense of living happily ever after fights with barely concealed feelings of obsessive sexuality and fanatical malice. When Lucretia
claims that this outcome was heaven's will, she reminds the audience that it is also their will. The play has hurdled us toward a conclusion that seems as inevitable as it is desirable. Our sympathy
has been enlisted on the side of an immoral plot whose resolution
is an ironic portrayal of separation *as* reconciliation.

So the play reestablishes among its characters a forward-
looking and apparently healthy community. The final scene is one
of the most intricate webs of dramatic irony ever spun on the
comic stage. It is as if the tone and structure of the opening lines of

the prologue have been dramatically realized in the members of this new miniature society. For one thing, the play now also proves itself to be a sort of ironic untaming of a shrew:

> MESSER NICIA. Lucretia, I believe it's good to do things in the fear of God, not like a mad woman.
> LUCRETIA. What's got to be done now?
> MESSER NICIA. See how she answers. She acts like a fighting cock.
> LUCRETIA. What are you trying to say?
> (5.6)

The final gathering of all the characters, similarly, is a theatrical image of reconciliation pervaded with crude double entendres and a tense, underlying sense of duplicity:

> MESSER NICIA. Do I see Ligurio and Doctor Callimaco in the church?
> FRATE. Yes, sir.
> MESSER NICIA. Beckon to them.
> FRATE. Come here.
> CALLIMACO. God be with you!
> MESSER NICIA. Doctor, let me present you to my wife.
> CALLIMACO. With pleasure.
> MESSER NICIA. Lucretia, this is the man who'll cause us to have a staff to support our old age.
> LUCRETIA. I'm delighted to meet him and want him to be our closest friend.
> MESSER NICIA. Now bless you. And I want him and Ligurio to come and have dinner with us this noon.
> LUCRETIA. Yes, indeed.
> MESSER NICIA. And I'm going to give them the key of the room on the ground floor of the loggia, so they can come there when it's convenient, because they don't have women at home and live like animals.
> CALLIMACO. I accept it, to use it when I like.
> (5.6)

Friends greet friends; God's blessing is invoked; the community rejoices in its continuity—and every line has a bawdy or ironic meaning. The polite "pleasure" of the social introduction becomes, for the audience, an image of desire triumphing over moral restrictions on it. Behind Nicia's hospitable offer of the civilized comfort of his house is a barely concealed image of bestial passion stampeding over order and restraint. These dramatic ironies overflow the boundaries of the play. Sostrata asks both the other characters and the audience, "who wouldn't be happy?"—and at this point, we are simply thrown back onto our own particular morality. Is this or isn't it a happy ending? The dramatic illusion converges with the veil of social hypocrisy in an image of impenetrable deceit.

Throughout the play, Machiavelli's subversive realism weighs moral value against moral actuality, testing his audience's sympathy with the latter, and inciting some critical discomfort over the next few centuries. *Mandragola* has been, for the most part, an admired, but not beloved play. For example, Elmer Edgar Stoll, writing in the middle years of our century, contrasts the "comic irony" of Machiavelli's "rank" comedy with Shakespeare's pastoral-lyrical-comical method, and concludes that in *Mandragola* "poet and spectator both have wry faces, or are exchanging waggish glances, as they part."[16] Stoll's disapproval is clear, but this image exactly conveys how the play creates a sort of cynical community both on stage and, finally, among the spectators. Machiavelli portrays a humanity united by its vices rather than by its values, suggesting we are no better than the people in his story—but no worse either. A historian and critic of the last century, in contrast, was deeply threatened by what he calls this "indecent" play:

> If we turn from the *Mandragola* to the society of which it is
> a study, and which complacently accepted it as an agreeable
> work of art, we are filled with a sense of surprise bordering on
> horror. . . . No one, at the date of its appearance, resented it.
> Florentine audiences delighted in its comic flavour. Leo X. witnessed it with approval. . . . Society, far from rising in revolt
> against the poet who exposed its infamy with a pen of poisoned
> steel, thanked the man of genius for rendering vice amusing.

Here is another critic drawn into melodramatic posturings by the spectacle of comedy's triumphant cynicism. And what the Italian Renaissance failed to deliver in moral outrage, John Addington Symonds was himself ready to supply:

> Viewed as a critique upon life, the *Mandragola* is feeble, because the premisses [*sic*] are false. . . . Men are not such fools as Nicia or such catspaws as Ligurio and Timoteo. Women are not such compliant instruments as Sostrata and Lucrezia [*sic*]. Human nature is not that tissue of disgusting meannesses and vices, by which Callimaco succeeds. . . . The world is not wholly bad; but in order to justify Machiavelli's conclusions, we have to assume that its essential forces are corrupt.[17]

Or do we? Symonds's commentary, like the play itself, throws us back onto our own particular beliefs about human nature. The scholar's insistence that these are *not* the conditions that prevail provides a fascinating contrast to the general critical judgment about Machiavelli's realism. The play embodies, thus, the essential ambiguity of cynicism itself, which is either a persistently negative tendency to degrade the world, or merely an unillusioned acceptance of its imperfection. Is *Mandragola* too realistic to be moral, or does it fail as realism because it fails as morality?

The *Mandragola,* like comedy itself, is built out of a tension of opposing visions of life, and everything the play expresses it seems also to question. It is the foolish Nicia, for example, who is allowed to express the personal sense of injustice and unrecognized merit that, as we know from the prologue, Machiavelli himself sincerely shared. "A man who doesn't have a pull with the government of this city," Nicia complains, "can't find a dog to bark at him, and we're good for nothing but to go to funerals and to meetings about some marriage, or to sit all day dawdling on the Proconsul's bench" (2.3). In the absence of the explicitly autobiographical prologue, a passage like this could convey the backward conservatism of the Saturnalia, for when a fool criticizes society for its failure to recognize his merit, we laugh in implicit reaffirmation of that society's basic sanity. But in this play we are implicitly reminded, instead, that the comedy we are in the process of enjoying was itself an ironic by-product of the inept social system that cut Machiavelli off from "showing other powers with other deeds." In Saturnalian comedy, as we have seen, a deliberately temporary indulgence in disorder serves as an ironic confirmation of good government; by contrast, Machiavelli seems to reverse this pattern to show that misrule is really the norm, that corruption prevails. But then he also shows us how the community muddles through, how what Symonds calls "the main forces of society" are somehow behind and separate from the official code of behavior.

For Lucretia—as for Symonds—there would be no distinction between social and personal constraints on behavior; the individual conscience and the injunctions of church or state would reflect and confirm one another. For Machiavelli, however, almost as it would later be for Brecht or Shaw, there is a kind of resiliency and wisdom in the human animal that is entirely untouched and unexplained by official codes of behavior. One of Brecht's most famous characters thanks God that human beings never live up to their own laws, concluding that "God is merciful and men are bribable, that's how His will is done on earth as it is in Heaven. . . . As long as there's corruption there'll be merciful judges and even the innocent may get off."[18] Machiavelli does not, perhaps, go so far. But he does conclude his play with a vivid image of a social situation created by fraud and defined by adultery, and he allows that situation to seem practical, permanent, and clearly preferable to the one it replaces. Machiavelli dramatizes how people manage to get what they want out of life while still preserving the appearance of a moral system that officially inhibits them. In the same way, his play concludes with a theatrical happy ending which conceals only partially the ironic turbulence of real life. *Mandragola*, like its characters, never seriously contradicts nor truly lives up to its own moral code. Perhaps we do rise from Machiavelli's comedy, in Stoll's words, exchanging "waggish glances" with the author, but we may also find ourselves wondering, as Frate Timoteo does, "which of us has bamboozled the other."

6 Middleton's Trick

In England, the business and the form of
comedy blossomed almost a hundred years
later than it had in Renaissance Italy, as
playwright and public alike enthusiastically jumped on the classical bandwagon and
created a new, definitive classic for audiences of the future. The Elizabethan and
Jacobean periods are, of course, the ones
with which every critic of drama must
finally come to terms. We must deal with
a corpus of drama whose greatness is in-
disputable, but also, perhaps, too often reaffirmed as merely such.
Still, the financial, material, and aesthetic success of the theatrical
enterprise over about a fifty-year span in England is certainly impressive. One cannot consider the repertoire of English comedy
without being struck by the diminution of its output after the clos-
ing of the theaters under the Commonwealth. The best-known
and most-highly regarded comic playwrights from the Restoration to Oscar Wilde averaged about four comedies apiece; Shakespeare produced somewhere between ten and eighteen, depending
on which generic standards we apply. No other period in the history of English comedy shows so striking a combination of artistic
and economic success. The progress of English comedy from the
clumsy and forced heartiness of *Ralph Roister Doister* (c. 1567)

to the sophisticated ironies of Jonson, Middleton, and their contemporaries in the early seventeenth century, was also what E. K. Chambers called a "progress towards that state of regulative security which, in the case of any industry dependent upon a permanent habitation and the outlay of capital, is the first condition of economic stability."[1] It was one of those magic periods in the history of culture when high artistic content and popular commercial appeal seem effortlessly to support one another.

Indeed, the "greatness" of Renaissance drama rests firmly upon the economic success of its producers. In his own day, for example, Shakespeare's financial achievement must have seemed little less impressive than his aesthetic one. Shakespeare was not only what we call the "greatest" dramatist of his age; he was also, among his fellow playwrights, apparently the best businessman. This son of a provincial bankrupt, this "upstart crow" of an actor turned playwright, managed to become a shareholder of the leading London theatrical company, and finally retired to Stratford as a self-remade gentleman. It is perhaps the most thorough success story in the history of the theater. Among Shakespeare's multitudinous talents there must have been a certain financial shrewdness. Certainly he had no romantic interest in starving for his art. The King's Men delivered a quality product for a reasonable price and their preeminent playwright rendered his services for cash and interest, producing plays—as far as he seems to have known or cared—that would be uncopied, unpublished, and unremembered.

Historians and critics remind us again and again that Shakespeare's age was one of social ferment: a transitional period between the feudal kingdom and the modern nation, and a time of growing crisis between old and new values. But the theater was a special kind of social phenomenon that, in both its content and its conditions, maintained an interested and interesting relationship with the overall pattern of social mobility and class conflict in Elizabethan and Jacobean society. Even an overview of this much-praised moment in English literary history reveals that same ambivalence toward drama in general and comedy in particular that we have met before, that same convergence of aesthetic and economic opinions. In the tradition of Puritan diatribe against the stage, the financial success of the players was always seen as a particular outrage. One Puritan sermonist in the late 1570s cites facts and figures to prove how lucrative the acting profession had become, and complains about the "great charges" with which the new bankside theaters had been built.[2] Stephen Gosson, in his well-known tract, *The School of Abuse* (1579), calls the theaters a "*market* of Bawdrie" (my emphasis), and claims that "some that have neither land to maintaine them, nor good occupation to get their bread, desirous to strowt it with the best, yet disdayning to live by the sweate of their browes, have found out this craft of Ledgerdemayne to play fast and loose among their neighbors."[3] Intoxicated with traditional images and themes, Gosson pictures the theater as a sort of con game or magical stage where a man is paid for mere playing; where these landless entertainers, these mountebanks, take on a reflected glamour and strut it as and with the best. Shakespeare too, in full literary self-consciousness, could meditate that the world was a stage; to Gosson and his fellow Puritans, in a different, yet strangely analogous sense, "playing" could also mean literal *acting* or simply *loose living,* and both were the converse of honest industry. The Puritans condemned the stage equally as mirror and as performance, arguing that the players "notoriously practice in real life the very vices which they represent on the stage."[4]

Of course, if the players embodied their own vices, they also embodied their own happy endings—many of them, as a certain tract observes, having "gone to London very meanly, and . . . come in time to be exceedingly wealthy." If nothing else, this is not a bad description of the playwright whose most famous character would extoll the players as the "abstract and brief chronicles of the time." The Elizabethans bequeathed to us a rhetorical treasure of splendid praise of, and savage invective against, the drama, both obviously inspired by its unparalleled achievements. The businessmen of the theater, engaged as they were in selling an intangible compound of spiritual and sensual pleasures, seem to have provoked a particular discomfort in a society still learning to accept capitalism in general. Puritans often associated the theater with prostitution, not always unjustly. We know, for example, that Phillip Henslowe, a celebrated entrepreneur of Elizabethan entertainment, was involved both in the Rose Theater and in several bankside houses of ill-repute.[5] And in any case, as George Bernard Shaw, a self-proclaimed modern puritan, would point out, even the greatest artists are also, in some sense, "pleasure merchants."[6]

There are also some ambivalent feelings about drama among the outstanding figures of the period. One of Shakespeare's most quoted passages, for example, is more than the piece of theatrical gossip for which it is often studied. I refer to that odd digression in the middle of *Hamlet,* in which Shakespeare allows Rosencrantz and Guildenstern to inform Prince Hamlet about the vogue for the children's companies then playing in the so-called private theaters. These "little eyases," says Rosencrantz, are engrossing the attention of theatergoers and cutting into the revenue of the "common stages." But the passage ends with a further bit of commentary that is of direct relevance neither to the whole play nor even to this already irrelevant and anachronistic discussion. When Rosencrantz explains, in a famous phrase, that the child-players are becoming more popular than even "Hercules and his load too"—evidently, the great Globe itself—Hamlet replies, "It is not very strange, for my uncle is King of Denmark, and those that would make mouths at him while my father liv'd, give twenty, forty, fifty, a hundred ducats a-piece for his picture in little. 'Sblood, there is something in this more than natural, if philosophy could find it out" (2.2.363–67).[7] So all this fashionable talk about the War of the Theatres and satire à la mode comes down, once again, to a question of money. Why should the face that yesterday provoked a sneer take on, through an arbitrary process of political authority and metallurgy, so grotesquely inflated a value? Shakespeare seems to be suggesting, through the twists and turns of Hamlet's antic disposition, that the children's theaters are the dross to the gold of his own art, and that the public's preference for the former is simply one more example of false values. As the face on the coin may be worth more than the face on the man, so the "aery of children" has turned the heads of the adult world. In this sense, the passage is also a mild contribution to the exchange of insult and innuendo between the public and private theaters that was a by-product of the more specific conflict between Jonson, Marston, and Dekker. A little controversy is always good for the box office: Rosencrantz claims that "there was for a while no money bid for argument unless the poet and the player went to cuffs in the question." But a passing preference for a new theatrical gimmick among London's theatergoing public is hardly comparable to the deeper human confusion of real versus financial values to which Hamlet also refers. Why were London theatergoers under Elizabeth and James so fascinated by capitalism in general and by the economic aspects of the theater in particular? This passage is not quite the compliment to Shakespeare's own audience that it appears to be.

And indeed, beneath the festive merriment of his plays, and despite his repeated intention to "please," Shakespeare does reveal a certain animosity toward his audience. George Bernard Shaw was not what we would call a disinterested critic of his great predecessor, but he is illuminating, at least, on the subject of Shakespeare's comic titles. In Shaw's playlet *The Dark Lady of the Sonnets,* the Bard complains to Queen Elizabeth that

> Only when there is a matter of a murder, or a plot, or a pretty youth in petticoats, or some naughty tale of wantonness, will your subjects pay the great cost of good players and their finery, with a little profit to boot. . . . I have writ these to save my friends from penury, yet shewing my scorn for such follies and for them that praise them by calling the one As You Like It, meaning that it is not as *I* like it, and the other Much Ado About Nothing, as it truly is.[8]

This imagined image of Shakespeare does not seem entirely implausible. And the titles of his comedies do change, in the course of his career, from the workmanlike classical simplicity of *The Comedy of Errors,* to the rather sarcastic and perfunctory *Twelfth Night: or What You Will,* and finally to the endlessly ironic, mock-proverbial *All's Well That Ends Well.* These titles themselves suggest two opposing attitudes: either the playwright is a pander, sincerely offering up comedy as his audiences liked it, or he is a condescending entertainer giving his audiences what they want and yet contemptuously suggesting they may call it what they will. In envisioning our own Shakespeare, we can

choose that egalitarian popular sentimentalist whom some critics
still celebrate and whom we can meet today in the souvenir shops
of Stratford-on-Avon, or that upwardly mobile bourgeois writer
who "regarded himself as a gentleman under a cloud . . . and
never for a moment as a man of the people,"[9] and whose "literary
attainments and successes were chiefly valued as serving the
prosaic end of making a permanent provision for himself and his
daughters."[10] This is our equivalent of an earlier pair of imagined
images of Shakespeare: the enduring myth that some aristocrat
was the true ghostwriter of the plays, versus the romantic legend
of a great artist "risen from the peasantry."[11]

In fact, in neither his lyric nor his dramatic modes did Shakespeare ever really unlock his heart, or reveal the genuine class
consciousness of, say, Ben Jonson. To me, his comedies communicate both more and less than the hopeful, "festive" vision of
a "new society," of fulfilled human community, which they seem
to announce and for which they are often praised. Shakespeare
chose, in comedy, to explore the innocent connections between
life and art embodied in his pun on "feigning" and "faining": the
secret identity of imagination and desire. The modern theater continues to devote frequent attention to these elegant concoctions
of prose realism around a lyrical core, these entertainments
transacted in symmetrical plots and in plays within the play.
Shakespeare mastered the genre, tested it, twisted it, and then
abandoned it: there are comic aspects of the final plays, but he
never really returned to the genre after *Hamlet.* Perhaps this is
because he could never quite believe in the comic image of final
reconciliation, nor entirely discard the utopian faith out of which
that image springs. In *As You Like It,* for example, Shakespeare
claims to be celebrating how "earthly things made even / Atone
together" (5.4.109–10). In fact, the perfunctory comic plot depicts a group of aristocrats enjoying a temporary (Saturnalian)
interlude in what critics call a "green world," a stylized forest
peopled with Arcadian yokels and associated with classless
images of the mythical Golden Age (1.1.119; 2.1.4). And out of
this pretended paradise comes no "new society," but simply a precise reestablishment of class (and sexual) distinctions. The love
games between Rosalind and Orlando, Phoebe and Silvius, seem

to center around issues of sexual identity and emotional matura-
tion; but Phoebe must be eventually persuaded to accept Silvius as
much for reasons of rank as for sexual preference. In the final
scene, as in the play generally, Shakespeare both denies and reaffirms the social hierarchy. At first, the masque of Hymen brings
the god of cities (5.4.146) to bless this make-believe pastoral, with
poetry celebrating the deep ties of nature that infuse human society and provide for its continuance. We are told only of an unspecified "eight that must take hands" in the "blessed bond of
board and bed"—as these couples now proceed to do, arms joined
in a seamless social circle. But then, after the messenger's speech
ties up the loose ends of the plot with a few fortuitous and wel-
come coincidences, Duke Senior announces that

> after, every of this happy company . . .
> Shall have the good of our returned fortune
> According to the measure of their states.
> (5.4.172–75)

Listen to the pale abstractions of the last line ring hollow before
these lovers poised to begin their dance. A few lines later, before
the audience hears, the Duke once again allows the symmetrical
lovers to form a deceiving image of "all nature in love":

> Mean time, forget this new fall'n dignity,
> And fall into our rustic revelry,
> Play, music, and you brides and bridegrooms all,
> With measure heap'd in joy, to the measures fall.
> (5.4.176–79)

The emotional distance conveyed in that phrase "mean time" is
characteristic of Shakespearean comedy.

The same double view of social class can be seen in other
aspects of Renaissance comedy, and it reflects, as we have suggested, the social half-light in which the players and playwrights
lived. Part of what was happening in the Renaissance was a
gradual institutionalization of the theater, a mingling of popular
and academic forms into a literature flexible enough to speak
alike to citizens and kings. But the courtly wit of a play like
Twelfth Night, one cannot forget, is deceptively far from the

social roots of its literary tradition. Throughout the period, the players who acted plays like it were still required to bind themselves as the servants of some nobleman or face possible prosecution under the Act of 1531 against vagrants and vagabonds. This notorious law—whose provisions bring us back, via real life, to Plautine images—declared that all "idle persons going about, some of them using divers and subtle crafty and unlawful games and plays . . . are punishable by whipping for two days together. For a second offense they are to be scourged two days and the third day to be put in the pillory from 9 to 11 in the forenoon and to have one of their ears cut off."[12] The macabre specificity of this and similar laws of the sixteenth century suggests some deep-seated social rage against the noneconomic person. At one end of the spectrum of comic *form* are the pratfalls of farce; at one end of comedy as a social product is this political assault on the human body. In any case, the various theatrical companies of the Renaissance became nominally "The Earl of Leicester's Men" or some such; and eventually, certain companies came to be sponsored by the queen or king. The players, thus, were in one sense mere servants, only a few social steps away from that vagabondage of which the Puritans continued to accuse them; yet they also had access to that world of art and privilege that has always defined itself by the manner and quality of its entertainments.

It is easy to forget, for example, that Ben Jonson was a brick-layer's son—precisely because, after the lucky chance of a classical education and some hard times with the patron and the jail, he finally came to consider himself a sort of aristocrat of letters who "demanded recognition . . . with a fearless assurance which sometimes strained the rigorous code of seventeenth-century etiquette."[13] Jonson was another great comic success story, yet, during the War of the Theatres, it was his pen that attacked the common stages with particular savagery. For him, the complexity of his art was a sort of social tool that separated the natural meritocracy of those who could appreciate it, from that "beast, the multitude" who cares only for "Theatricall wit, right Stage-jesting, and relishing a Play-house."[14] Throughout his career, Jonson shows the Horatian contempt of audiences, and he alternately damned and mocked

> The wise, and many-headed Bench, that sits
>   Upon the Life, and Death, of *Playes* and *Wits*,
> Composed of *Gamester, Captain, Knight, Knight's man*,
>   *Lady* or *Pusil*, that weares maske or fan,
> *Velvet* or *Taffeta* cap, ranked in the darke
>   With the shops Foreman, or some such *brave sparke*
> That may judge for his *sixpence*.[15]

In this fascinating passage, the spectators become stock characters from some larger Comedy of Manners; they are "ranked," lined-up side by side in the darkness of the indoor private theaters, and that same darkness conceals their social "rank." Jonson's snobbery moves between aesthetic and social prejudices, and he maintains an imperious distance from audiences and fellow playwrights alike:

> Though neede make many Poets, and some such
> As art, and nature have not better'd much;
> Yet ours, for want, hath not so lov'd the stage,
> As he dare serve th'ill customes of the age:
> Or purchase your delight at such a rate,
> As, for it, he himselfe must justly hate.[16]

Notice the sneer at the poet who writes for "need," and the inversion which has Jonson purchasing the audience's "delight" instead of, as really happens, selling it to them.

   The other playwright we are going to consider probably did write plays out of real financial necessity; we find, in fact, that Jonson once called him a "base fellow" who "was not of the number of the Faithfull, Poets."[17] For all that, Thomas Middleton's father happens also to have been a bricklayer, one who died early enough and with a sufficiently large estate to leave his widow, his stepfather, and young Thomas quarreling over it for some years. The playwright's interest in the theme of inheritance, thus, may be more than conventional. Middleton was born in 1580 and by 1601 was "daylie accompaninge the players."[18] It was the beginning of a long career as a journeyman-dramatist who turned out plays in a wide variety of genres for more than twenty years and yet who remained for his contemporaries, as for us, in T. S. Eliot's elegiac phrases, "inscrutable, solitary, unadmired; welcoming collaboration, indifferent to fame."[19] In the first years of the seventeenth century, Middleton developed what is probably his most significant contribution to the drama of the period: a kind of cynical and sophisticated comic play set in a believable contemporary London. Middleton's characters make their comic pilgrimage not through a Shakespearean green world, but through an urban underworld. He was not the only exponent of what is sometimes called "city comedy" or "citizen comedy," but not even Ben Jonson, whose moral complexities and finely wrought dramatic textures earn him a larger place in the history of the drama, conveys such a convincing sense of locale and social detail. Middleton was from a background of middle-class respectability, yet he evidently knew poverty and low life equally well—"the streets, the inns, the dark alleyways by the river, the haunts of watermen."[20] For most of critical history, it was generally agreed that Middleton was the greatest "realist" in Jacobean comedy.[21] We will be looking at some of the attempts made by modern critics to pinpoint the precise social attitudes conveyed by the plays and the playwright. But in my own view, Middleton evokes a vision of moral and social turmoil which he is unwilling or unable to resolve into coherence. His plays are filled with social prejudices and attitudes, with intimations of moral judgment, and the conflicts of class with class that he depicts are resolved into apparent order. But Middleton's theatrical effects obscure the conflict and the victory: he takes sides only after the play, and between the lines.

There is even something paradoxical about Middleton's much-vaunted realism. At one time or another, Middleton produced plays for virtually all the major theatrical companies, but most of his city comedies, including A Trick to Catch the Old One, which we will look at in detail, were written for the "little eyases," specifically the Children of Paul's. Thus one of the most naturalistic of Renaissance comedies was written for actors whose actual age and appearance would necessarily enforce an absolute distance between them and the story they enacted. The private theaters were more expensive to attend, and they purveyed a generally more sophisticated and spicier fare than their adult counterparts. Their audiences too may have been of somewhat greater education and social rank. At least, the playwrights of the private theaters who attacked the "drunken rout" of common spectators have made us think so. Certainly the plays performed by the children, including Middleton's, do exploit the upper-class prejudices of the time, finding their characteristic comic target in citizens, Puritans, and the petit bourgeois. *A Trick* portrays the conflict between a landed but bankrupt gentleman and the New Men of the City, enacted in the no-man's-land between inherited rank and acquired class, the battleground where fortunes were made and misdirected. Like so many later playwrights who would also deal with social mobility and its consequences, Middleton focuses on the deceptiveness of appearances within a society whose forms and institutions no longer convey their traditional meaning.

In one sense, however, the children must have already embodied this theme in the conditions of their performances. Part of the special spice of the private theater entertainments must have been to see children transformed into the pimps, prostitutes, and sophisticated men and women about town who enact plays like Middleton's. In a play such as *Twelfth Night,* which was performed by adult players at the Globe, there is something childlike about the aristocratic characters who play-act their quietly implausible story in that comic never-never land, Illyria. Middleton, by contrast, creates for his preadolescent actors a gallery of worldly wise Londoners who seem, even today, entirely adult in their attitudes and appetites. These extremely precocious and talented children must have always embodied a certain satire on the human condition—an implicit comic debate of innocence versus experience. The children were themselves emblems of the social transformations they mocked on the stage. In the 1590s, Shakespeare's Theseus generously pardons the dramatic ineptitude of the comical tragedy performed in honor of his wedding:

> The best in this kind are but shadows, and the worst
> are no worse, if imagination amend them.
> (*A Midsummer Night's Dream,* 5.1.211–12)

Less than ten years later, a character from Middleton would echo these famous phrases in a new social context, expressing a different view of the relation between imagination and appearance: "what base birthe does not rayment make glorious? and what glorious births do not ragges make infamous? why should not a woman confesse what she is now? since the finest are but deluding shadowes, begot betweene Tyrewomen and Taylors?" (*Michaelmas Term*, 2.1.2–6).[22] The Elizabethan infatuation with theatrical illusion is translated into a partly cynical, partly celebratory declaration that, in real life too, people are not always what they seem.

A Trick to Catch the Old One opens, similarly, with its main character expressing his own complicated sense of what he is, what he has become, and what he still can be. "All's gone!" cries Theodorus Witt-good as the play opens, "Still, thou'rt a Gentleman, that's all; but a poore one, that's nothing" (1.1.1–2).[23] The turns of this little piece of rhetoric express the familiar ambiguity of social attitude. In the first half of the sentence, Witt-good seems to be saying to himself that, since his estate is gone, he is now "a Gentleman, that's all"—in other words, he now has merely the name and form of a social condition whose reality requires a material wealth he has squandered. The second half of the sentence, where we might expect some phrase in apposition, gives us, instead, a surprising antithesis: "*but* a poor one, that's nothing." Now the whole sentence expresses the same idea we have just paraphrased; but the words we took to mean *merely* a gentleman stand in a new relation to the rest of the sentence, which now means: you will always be a gentleman, which is *all-important*, even though you're poor. It is the poverty that is "nothing," of no consequence—and in fact the play will demonstrate Witt-good's impressive ability to regain his inheritance. With the same concision we have seen at other crucial moments in dramatic comedy, Witt-good's line embodies the social dilemma: is it the names and forms of social distinction that matter, or is it rather true (as Charlie Chaplin would remark of America, centuries later), that one can be whatever class one can afford to be?[24] In self-mocking soliloquy, Witt-good dwells on the familiar comic conflict between lust and loot:

What milk brings thy Meadowes forth now? where are Thy
goodly Up-lands and thy Downe-lands, all sunke into that little
pitte Lecherie? why should a Gallant pay but two shillings for
his Ordnary that nourishes him, and twenty times two for his
Brothell that consumes him? but where's Long-acre? in my
Uncle's conscience, which is three yeares voyage about; he that
setts out upon his conscience, nere finds the way home again.
(1.1.3–8)

As Witt-good sees it, money both nourishes and consumes:
emerging out of the life-giving land only to disappear into human
appetite; elevating a man into gentility yet also sinking him into
the quicksand of avarice and self-interest. Witt-good's uncle not
only values money more than the ties of family and affection, like
Shylock and all stage usurers before and after him; he has even, we
now learn, defined a "principle in usury" which turns these traditional human bonds inside out:

> Hee that doth his youthe expose,
> To Brothell, drinke, and danger,
> Let him that is his neerest Kinne,
> Cheate him before a Stranger.
> (1.1.14–17)

Thus the play is intended, we might easily assume, to heal the
social disorder represented by Witt-good's dilemma and his
uncle's avarice. We watch this penniless but attractive young man
mocking the uncle who, with what the audience presumably finds
a callous disregard for humanity, has usurped the estate that defines Witt-good's position as "still a Gentleman." In this opening
scene, in other words, we are seeing an apparent victim strike
back at his oppressor with a kind of gallows humor—a verbally
triumphant wit that refuses to suffer his own conscience or his
uncle's lack thereof. Witt-good stands here in the position of the
Plautine trickster slave, and we are inevitably on his side in our
anticipation of his "trick," which we know will both entertain us
and succeed in its objectives. But here, it is not the principle,
simply the money, that is at stake. The rest of the play will show
how Witt-good himself cheats his "neerest Kinne" and various

other people, abandoning his mistress for a rich woman along the
way. In this opening scene, we are led to believe that the outrageous injustice of Witt-good's uncle will be defeated and rectified by the play. In fact, Witt-good succeeds in regaining his estate
and acquiring new wealth by whole-heartedly adopting the self-
interested attitude of New Men like Lucre and Hoord—and bet-
tering the instruction.

But after all, as Witt-good proceeds to ask himself and us, "how
should a man live now, that ha's no living; hum?" His pun both
enforces and contradicts the ultimate identity of money and life,
and raises a question that must genuinely have troubled some of
Middleton's contemporaries, perhaps also the playwright himself. Witt-good answers with another question that seems to identify him with that particular class of men who, lacking land and
occupation, turned to that craft that makes them of special interest to us today: "why are there not a million men in the world, that
onely sojourne upon their brains, and make their wittes their
Mercers?" (1.1.22–24). As the pamphlet literature of the age suggests, Jacobean London had its share of literal con artists—the
coney-catchers, projectors, and so forth. But the players and the
playwrights obviously also could be said to live on their wits—
and to the Puritans and moralists, there seemed little difference
between any of these new ways to make money. To Middleton,
we are seeing, there may have been some connection between his
character and himself. Shakespeare too was fond of the suggestive
paradox to which he gave a perfect rhetorical symmetry: "The
truest poetry is the most feigning" (*As You Like It*, 3.3.19).
And Shakespeare always suggests some connection between this
mysterious nature of art and the analogous "feigning" of his characters who play-act their way to self-knowledge and love. In this
opening scene of *A Trick*, Middleton fills the speech of Witt-good
and his nameless "Curtizan" lover with the same images of disguise and game, the same motif of life-as-theater, that are so
familiar to us from Shakespearean comedy, but that are here
placed into a disturbing new context. The courtesan promises to
give Witt-good "whatever lies within the power of my performance" (1.1.50), and even the double entendre may remind us of
other witty heroines from happier comedies. A few lines later,

preparing to "take the name and forme" of "a rich country wid-
dow," the courtesan predicts

> I will so art-fully disguise my wants
> And set so good a courage on my state,
> That I will be beleeved.
> (1.1.74–75)

Then Witt-good himself goes off to deceive his friend, the
"Hoste," whose aid they will require, "with the best Art, and
most profitable form" (96). The situation is reminiscent of plays
like *Twelfth Night* or *As You Like It:* lovers disguising themselves and describing their project with images of sexuality and
procreation:

> WITT-GOOD. . . . what Trick is not an Embrion at first, until
> a perfect shape come over it.
> CURTIZAN. Come I must helpe you, where abouts left you, I'll
> proceed.
> Though you beget, tis I must help to breed,
> Speak what ist, Ide faine conceave it.
> (52–58)

For Shakespeare, as we have observed, the process of love was itself a kind of role-playing by which lovers paradoxically come to a
deeper and truer understanding of themselves and their beloved.
With Witt-good and his lover, however, their motives are financial rather than personal; and their mutual disguise, instead of
bringing them to renewed affection, will result in their complete
and final separation.

The rest of the play seems to exemplify, almost too obviously,
what Northrop Frye has called the "comic Oedipal situation," in
which "a *senex iratus* . . . gives way to a young man's desires."[25]
Middleton's two young lovers will manage to catch not one but
two "old ones" with a trick that apparently embodies the conventional comic conflict of youth and age, generous vitality and bar-
ren avarice. But despite the youth of Middleton's protagonists,
and the age of their antagonists, despite even the title, which virtually shouts this apparent theme at its audience, the play isn't really
about the generation gap, and it certainly doesn't give us the con-

ventional comic vision of human continuity between the generations. It is true that both Lucre and Hoord are typical blocking characters who obviously represent the ascendancy of greed over genuine human bonds of loyalty and love. And they are both, as we expect, hoist with their own petard, defeated by their own obsessive need to substitute financial for familial relationships. Lucre is deceived into returning Witt-good's estate by the hope of robbing more from him; while Hoord is duped into marrying the courtesan whom he takes for the rich widow she pretends to be. But the final victory of these young characters cannot be said to bring any sense of social renewal or clarification. Middleton's comic resolution, conversely, seems to take his characters one step further from a society whose ties are personal and loving, one step closer to the social dominance of money and self-interest. In one scene, Lucre pretends to offer his nephew a familial hospitality when he hears of his supposed prospects for a wealthy marriage; when Witt-good refuses the invitation, the old man muses, "see what tis when a mans come to his lands" (2.1.78). Later, when Lucre actually does return the mortgage to Witt-good, Middleton puns on a word with dual personal and financial senses:

> LUCRE. . . . you know I give it you but in trust.
> WITT-GOOD. Pray let me understand you rightly, Uncle, you give it me but in trust.
> LUCRE. No.
> WITT-GOOD. That is, you trust me with it.
> LUCRE. True, true.
> WITT-GOOD. (*Aside*) But if ever I trust you with it agen, would I might be trust up for my labour.
> (4.4.64–71)

Consider, by contrast, how in *As You Like It* it is only the usurper Duke Frederick who tears father from daughter, friend from friend, and that play, of course, depicts the usurper's defeat and the reconciliation of his victims. Here, Witt-good regains his lands and his rank by humiliating his uncle, robbing his creditors, and marrying his mistress and accomplice to a greedy and ridiculous old man. Witt-good himself marries a young woman for whom his most extreme expression of affection anywhere in the play is the ambiguous promise to be "still the same that I was in love" (3.3.19). As far as I can see, this play merely depicts the defeat of "realistically" greedy characters—financiers and usurers from contemporary London—by an equally greedy young wit who acquires an apparently higher moral status in our eyes simply because his methods are so entertaining and his victory so absolute.

The curious scenes depicting the life and death of that other usurer, Dampit, about whom critics have never felt comfortable, can thus be taken as a miniature version of the whole play. In Dampit's final appearance, we see a dying scoundrel surrounded by his no-less repulsive friends who torment him and recite unconvincing platitudes about the inevitable damnation of all usurers. Perhaps Middleton did intend the audience to draw some kind of moral lesson from this inorganic and incomplete subplot, but whatever his intentions, Dampit's story is in fact what one critic aptly calls a "safety valve for disgust."[26] Only by contrast to these grotesque scenes can the main part of the play take on even a semblance of comic festivity.

So Middleton, like the other comic playwrights we have considered, lets his audience have it both ways. He exploits the contemporary prejudice against the acquisitive instincts of the New Men, and yet concludes his play with an ending whose happiness is a pure triumph of financial acquisition. A play about *getting* ends with Witt-good formally "giving away" his old vices. But we know from the first scene that, in any case, Witt-good is already surfeited with his "follyes" quite specifically because he has found them too expensive. And "giving away" his vices also means "giving away" the courtesan—whose devotion to Witt-good is the only genuine affection I can find in this play, and whom Witt-good now blithely relinquishes with a bawdy joke or two. Thus Witt-good, having claimed what he wants, can now safely boast of being himself "reclaymd." And it is characteristic of Middleton's duplicity that even the concluding moral litany is expressed in a doggerel verse that, besides recalling the rhyming "principle of usury" we heard at the beginning, does not convey even a pretense of serious morality.

Notwithstanding all this, modern critics seems to be able to find a moral vision in the play by also finding a genuine moral value in its protagonist. For example, George Rowe argues that both Witt-good and the courtesan are "morally superior to all of the other characters."[27] David Holmes claims, similarly, that "Witt-good's moral condition begins to improve in the course of the play, and it is this improvement that justifies his success."[28] Both these writers make much of Witt-good's treatment of his lover, and they both cite the same passage in describing how Witt-good's "generous feeling somewhat mollifies the fierce selfishness of his motives."[29] We know that the courtesan readily agreed to assist Witt-good in his scheme, but the young man's intentions toward her are, at first, not entirely clear. We do not even know precisely how Witt-good had originally intended to regain his estate from Lucre, though presumably the idea was that Lucre would help Witt-good win the rich widow in the hope of later usurping this new estate along with the old one. As Lucre puts it, after hearing of Witt-good's prospects: "if it come to a peece of mony I will not greatly sticke fort, there may be hope some of the widdowes lands too, may one day fall upon me if things be carried wisely" (2.1.167–69). Almost immediately, however, this supposedly rich widow attracts other suitors, including Lucre's enemy Hoord— who sees in the prospect of marrying her not only a financial triumph for himself, but also a way of discomfiting the other two men. And when Witt-good learns of this, he immediately sees a way of taking care of the courtesan and thus tying up a potentially loose end of the plot. Here then, is Witt-good instructing the courtesan to encourage Hoord's suit, in words that have inspired such generous approbation from modern critics:

> Wench, make up thy fortunes now, do thy selfe a good turne once in thy Dayes, hees rich in money, moveables, and lands, marry him, he's an old doting foole, and thats worth all, marry him, twould bee a great comfort to me to see thee do well ifaith, —marry him twould ease my conscience well to see thee well bestowd, I have a care of thee ifaith. (3.1.113–19)

With remarkable unselfishness, Witt-good gives his permission to the courtesan to marry the old doting fool so that, as he frankly admits, he may ease his conscience. Witt-good is still a gentleman and the courtesan has caught a credulous husband; both facts, re-

calling the opening lines of the play, are "worth all," yet they are
not precisely equivalent achievements. If, as some will suggest, it
is impossible to expect the young man to marry his whore, it is
also impossible to commend his sympathy and concern. Listen to
the nervous rhythms and repetitions in the passage convey a sense
of eager duplicity. A profusion of pronouns—"marry *him* . . . I
have a care of *thee*"—suggests the self-interest underlying this
passage of supposed generosity. One of Middleton's modern
editors, commenting on this same moment in the play, goes to
remarkable lengths to prove Witt-good's altruism: "It is to be
noted that Witt-good voluntarily shelves his project of tricking
Lucre into returning the mortgage, in fact, dangerously imperils
the plan, in order that the Curtizan may be assured of wealth and
respectability."[30] But it is hard to see how the courtesan's marriage imperils the success of the trick in any sense: Witt-good is
expecting "goodness to me by it" just lines after he learns of it. In
any case, what actually does happen, and what the audience
therefore sees, is that the courtesan's marriage plays directly into
Witt-good's scheme. Witt-good uses the impending marriage to
provoke Lucre into returning the entire mortgage at a stroke, so
that he may win back the widow's esteem and estate; and then,
claiming a legal precontract with her, he dupes Hoord into paying
off his debts.

It is finally to Middleton's ironic credit, I would argue, that
critics still contrive to find a moral vision in a play that portrays
and partly endorses an unrestrained individualism. It is a mark of
the perverse effectiveness of "city comedy" in general that it is still
interpreted as antibourgeois—since such plays so thoroughly affirm the bourgeois ideology of self-interest. But then, as we have
learned even more clearly in our own times, the desire to affront
the middle class is itself middle class. This contradiction is at the
heart of *A Trick to Catch the Old One*—and, as most of the play's
critics have more or less explicitly recognized, the play remains
deeply divided in purpose and character. T. S. Eliot saw in Middleton a conflict between the desire to "please his audience," and
his "steady impersonal passionless observation."[31] A more recent
critic suggests a different opposition, arguing that Middleton
"wants to portray realistically and even cynically a world peopled

only by successful scoundrels . . . and he also wants to portray
a well ordered world . . . in which scoundrels, no matter how
clever they may be, are in the end invariably brought to justice."[32]
Notice that these two definitions of Middleton's personal dialectic do not correspond in any simple way. Middleton pleased his
audience both with his cynical realism—which provides a titillating, implicitly flattering sense of sophistication—*and* with the
moral pretense that Theodorus Witt-good somehow "deserves"
his success. The audience is indulged both with the official moral
position and with an amusingly cynical attack on official morality. "Middleton's comic world . . . has two polarities," says R. B.
Parker, "a completely amoral vitalism and a more than Calvinisti-
cally-determined scheme of retribution."[33] This opposition is like
a mirror image of the one that Mikhail Bakhtin discovered in
Renaissance realism: that conflict between the "ever-laughing
principle of renewal" and the "inertia of class society." Each of
these critics uses broadly analogous terms, but places the moral
value on a different side of the equation. But in fact, if there is
"retribution" in *A Trick*, it is a retribution demanded by "amoral
vitalism" from itself. Witt-good revenges himself upon Lucre, but
then the playwright forces him to kneel down and repent his own
liveliness. In this sense, perceivable even beneath the self-cancel-
ing ironies I have tried to describe, the play is still firmly in the
Saturnalian tradition. But the real trick of this play is how Middleton manages to flatter both our fears and our hopes: to indulge
our prejudices even as he makes us uncomfortably aware of their
absurdity. Middleton restores rather than renews; he depicts
reconciliation as merely the mirror and consequence of separation. Thus this serviceable and lively stage play is finally a maimed
comedy, yet it also takes on a final ironic shape for us even as we
recognize its moral inadequacies. We enjoy the play's pyrotechni-
cal cynicism even though we know it may blow up in our faces,
even though we too may be hoist with our own petard. In this
play, Witt-good gets what he wants, and we get the joke.

Three

Comedy and Faith:

A Transcendent History

7 The Play and the World

Madame, you're making history. In fact, you're
making me.
GROUCHO MARX, *Monkey Business*

It is often said that Euripides was the first
"realistic" playwright, but to a modern
audience he could seem so only by comparison with his forebears on the Greek
tragic stage. Aeschylus and Sophocles
could not have been easy acts to follow for
any playwright, and to my mind, the alleged Euripidean "realism" was really a
kind of self-consciousness about theatrical
tone and genre. In the *Helen*, for example,
Euripides turns public tragedy into private
comedy. As he retells the familiar story, Paris stole from Greece
not the real princess, but a counterfeit image of her constructed by
Hera—so that Helen's phantom honor was, in fact, the honor of
a phantom. In the course of the play, Menelaus finally realizes he
has been "swindled by the gods,"[1] and that the whole protracted
slaughter at the gates of Ilium was all a sort of divine practical
joke. As the ghost-Helen taunts:

> Wretched men of Troy
> and all you Achaeans who, day after day, went on
> dying for me beside Scamander, by Hera's craft,
> you thought Paris had Helen, when he never did.
> (609–12)

Or, as Menelaus's servant asks, less poetically:

> You mean
> it was for a cloud, for nothing, we did all that work?
> (703–4)

But Euripides proceeds somehow to transform this cosmic irony into the comic ironies of his "light elegant romance."[2] Prior to the opening of the play, the gods had brought the real Helen to Egypt, and as the play begins, the Egyptian king Theoclymenus is seeking to marry her. When Menelaus coincidentally is shipwrecked and washed ashore in this very place, Helen convinces Theoclymenus that he is only a servant bringing the news of her husband's death. Then Helen contrives to escape from Egypt under the pretense of performing his funeral ritual at sea. Thus in the background of this story is that grand misapprehension that launched a thousand ships, but in the foreground are the comic misapprehensions of Helen's ingenious plot:

> THEOCLYMENUS. Now, do not waste yourself with too much weeping.
> HELEN. No.
> Today will show the quality of my love for you.
> (1418–20)

Observing the total situation of this play, it is as though Euripides made a cruel myth even crueler in order to wrench some reconciliation from it. Emotionally the play balances specific happiness against general woe, the individual longing for love against the myriad separations of real history.

This revised version of Helen's story suggests why Sophocles reportedly said that he drew men as they ought to be, Euripides, as they are,[3] and why modern scholars agree that Euripides paved the way for the bourgeois New Comedy of the next generation. Certainly Helen is a far-more vulnerable and familiar character than, say, Oedipus; yet the former's good fortune is as unreasonable as the latter's punishment. If the *Helen* is not precisely a comedy, it does reveal the characteristic double comic motion toward realistic satire and idealizing fantasy. On the one hand, Euripides' implausible distortion of the events of the Trojan War is in part intended to be an oblique sermon on real war: an ironic demonstration that all men who fight are really fighting for a phantom. As the chorus puts it:

> Mindless, all of you, who in the strength of spears
> and the tearing edge win your valors
> by war, thus stupidly trying
> to halt the grief of the world . . .
> By hate they won the chambers of Priam's city;
> they could have resolved by reason and words
> the quarrel, Helen, for you.
> (1152–55; 1158–60)

It is perhaps in this moral sense that Menelaus most represents men "as they are" in real life. On the other hand, the structure of the play does impart a special quality to these lovers who stand at the center of an anterior tragedy and yet escape from it into romantic comedy. They are both larger and smaller than their story: they embody a parable on the uselessness of conflict, but also a human drama whose fortunate resolution seems to make sense of the conflict from which it stems. At the weary end of a war much chronicled in literature and history, its audience is treated to a final, peripheral happy ending, as these two endearingly faithful lovers are reunited in a ballet of coincidence and deception.

Thus, as so often in comedy, the characters are more "realistic" than the plot, but even their familiarity seems merely provisional. Menelaus wears rags and is comically humbled by a female servant, and Helen speaks convincingly of her believable sorrows. For a brief theatrical moment, the two characters escape the mythic dimensions of their roles and become fallible human beings enacting a "realistic" comedy. But their personal happy ending proves also to be part of a divine plan; and in their common fate they once again become emblems, factors in a cosmic equation. For when Theoclymenus decides to pursue the fleeing lovers, Helen's divine half brothers appear in the sky to explain

> We would have saved our sister long ago, since Zeus
> had made us into gods and we had power, except

that we were weaker still than destiny, and less
than all the gods, whose will was these things should be.
(1658–62)

The divine purpose is apparently not merely that Troy must burn,
or that the lovers must escape—since these dei ex machina could
have reunited them long ago. Destiny decrees, in effect, that there
be a play. Helen and Menelaus must earn their own redemption,
not only because (as Euripides was certainly not the first to point
out) God helps those that help themselves (*Alcestis* 383), but
also because, in so doing, they make drama for us. The theatrical
self-consciousness of this play intersects and qualifies its apparent
moral vision. If Euripides does examine the general through the
particular, as Aristotle and the classical tradition argued all fiction
must do, he does so only to evoke a troubling incongruity between
the individual human destiny and the larger pattern of history.
The *dioscuri* dismiss Theoclymenus and the audience, concluding
that

> Heaven never hates the noble in the end.
> It is for the nameless multitude that life is hard.
> (1678–79)

The normal irony of a comic resolution is that a happy ending is
the opposite of what the events of the play give us any right to expect. In these lines, Euripides goes even further, asserting in mock-
proverbial manner that his wish-fulfilling happy ending is indeed
a typical case—of the world's injustice. The *Helen*, apparently
diverging widely from what "really" happened to its characters,
actually mirrors and confirms the unequal distribution of good
fortune in our social order. Thus the play dooms itself to irony:
the playwright seems to remake the world in favor of the individual, but then asks us to accept Helen's second honeymoon as
sufficient recompense for the numberless sufferings of an invisible
multitude. Perhaps what Euripides did contribute to the history of
comedy was not simple realism, but this sense of ironic incongruity between the play and the world, between comic verisimilitude
and the social reality outside the theater—or, in other words, the

happy ending contrived in exception to the rule, the fortunate
resolution enacted in spite of history.

"If you believe our civilization is founded in common sense,"
writes George Meredith at a much later point, "you will, when
contemplating men, discern a spirit overhead." Surveying the
antics of this "comic spirit" over some two and one-half millen-
nia, Meredith seems to ignore his own broad perspective when he
concludes that "Man's future upon earth does not attract it." As
Meredith envisions him, the classical features of this benevolent
demigod seem as baroque as they do Hellenic:

> It has the sage's brows, and the sunny malice of a faun lurks at
> the corners of the half-closed lips drawn in an idle wariness of
> half tension. That slim feasting smile, shaped like the long bow,
> was once a big round satyr's laugh, that flung up the brows like
> a fortress lifted by gunpowder. The laugh will come again, but
> it will be of the order of the mind, finely-tempered, showing
> sunlight of the mind, mental richness rather than noisy
> enormity.[4]

We can see here, at the exhausted close of the classical tradition,
how the Euripidean judge and disposer, descending ex machina to
deliver the happy ending and reopen within the story a sense of fu-
turity and history, has become a painted figure of the drawing
room, a creature of elvin mischief snatching the chair from under
the pompous burgher. Meredith's spirit does not descend: he is
a spectator filling the *theatrum mundi* with polite, "silvery
laughter," or a stagehand directing an "oblique light" on his leading ladies and gentlemen. But this satyric creature also possesses
an uncanny resemblance to Socrates—who, recalling what critics
teach us about the Aristophanic clash of *eiron* and *alazon* (the
ironist who exposes the imposter), appears for our culture both as
the *alazon* of *The Clouds*, and as the martyred *eiron* of our whole
civilization. Wylie Sypher has eloquently summarized his significance within the comic tradition:

> The essential character of the *eiron* is incarnate in Socrates,
> who was "ignorant" and who also had the disposition of the

"buffoon" or "fool," the features of the comic spirit itself, the
coarse, ugly mask of the satyr or clown. The Socratic method is
a tactic of winning victory by professing ignorance, by merely
asking questions to the "imposters," the so-called "wise" men
of Athens. Irony "defeats the enemy on his own ground," for in
the course of the comic debate the supposed wisdom of the
alazon is reduced to absurdity, and the *alazon* himself becomes
a clown. Thus Socrates, without risking any dogmatic answers,
corrects the folly of those sophists who claimed to know the
truth, or who were ignorant enough to presume there is no
truth. So the ironical man by his shrewd humility ("lying low
beneath the gods and saying nothing") proves to be wiser than
the wisdom of the world.[5]

Meredith invites us to question his own argument with this satyric
and Socratic comic spirit: for Socrates represents no complacent
affirmation of our social health, no comfortably conservative indifference to the future. Socrates embodies the power of irony and
the simplicity of truth: a skepticism at once philosophic and
comical.

Consider the characteristic doubleness of Meredith's essay: he
tries to extol comedy, yet he actually limits its scope and potential
by seeing it, with the classical critics of an earlier age, as merely
corrective therapy for our individual neuroses. Or, as we may
choose to see it, Meredith tries to diminish comedy's power and
yet reveals a tacit understanding of that power. It is one more
example of the ambiguity of the critical response to comedy. We
have seen the Renaissance critics distort Aristotle's moral vision
of comic character with a class bias that fails even to reflect the
true social dimensions of the living drama. Here, Meredith out-
does the classicists, straining to express his aristocratic image of
comedy in democratic terms. "A perception of the Comic Spirit
gives high fellowship," he argues. "You become a citizen of the
selecter world, the highest we know of in connection with our old
world. . . . Look there for your unchallengeable upper class!"[6]
Earlier, Meredith had inverted the classical idea that comic characters are lower class, but now he brings back the Aristotelian
ethical dimension, ranking comic audiences and characters

together, high in the hierarchy of wit. From "worse than," to socially "lower than," comic characters become with Meredith the comic reflection of their urbane and civilized audiences—"gentlemen," as Dryden put it, who are "entertained with the follies of each other."[7] In a critical argument largely focusing on the works of Molière, comedy has become a "high" genre whose basic locus is the library and the drawing room. Only from such sheltered and comfortable perspectives does comedy seem to express the will of a united society, the prevailing and present conditions of social life.

Oddly enough, however, Meredith's particular vision of comedy is tailor-made to *Le Misanthrope*, at once the most celebrated and most eccentric of Molière's plays. This is a comedy whose central lovers are never reunited, and in which, as Goethe remarked, "there is presented to our sight and to our attention that which has often impelled us to despair and threatened to drive us . . . from society."[8] *Le Misanthrope* invites two symmetrical and contradictory interpretations: either Alceste is the comic butt of a play that affirms the common sense of a society united against him, or, as Goethe suggests, he is a nearly tragic figure whose uncompromising moral position represents a profound attack on society and its basic premises. And thinking back to Helen and Menelaus, or to some of the uncountable other Jacks and Jills who enact similar plots and plays on later stages, overcoming external obstacles and inner differences to achieve the reconciliation that Molière denies to Alceste and Celimene, we can see both illustrations and refutations of Meredith's insistence that comedy does not deal with the future. True enough, the divine purpose in the *Helen*, like a playwright's purpose generally, is that there be a play; each joke, each turn of comic phrase, each *qui pro quo* of mistaken meaning, transpires in a particular here and now for the audience and the characters, both within the literal performance and within the comic mirror. "Take the present time," the comic spirit frequently advises, "Present mirth hath present laughter." In most comedies, however, we are also assured that the lovers whose perturbations and despair are the play will live happily ever after. The characters misstep through a comic present, within a plot that propels them toward the future. It is really the tragic, not the comic vision, that holds posterity up to question and demands of the catastrophe, as one character does during the horrific final scene of *King Lear,* "is this the promised end?"

> The oldest hath borne much; we that are young
> Shall never see so much, nor live so long.
> (5.3.326–27)

For the tragic images of apocalypse and doomsday, most comedies substitute images of procreation and abiding love, affirming the continuity of the human community from generation to generation.

Modern criticism has come to accept that an ironic union of tragedy and comedy is contained within some of the greatest works of either. As seasons join to form the natural order, it is argued, so tragedy and comedy join in a larger and more complex vision. Socrates, too, was a doomed tragic figure of his own present, whose living presence in history is a comic triumph over the judicial imposters and the cup of hemlock. Comedy is, as anthropological observation or mere metaphor, the "completed ritual"—the Feast that follows the Sacrifice.[9] "Tragedy and comedy," writes F. M. Cornford, "have the same divine protagonist, the dying God whose defeat is a victory, the ironical Buffoon whose folly confounds the pretence of wisdom."[10] "The tragic story," writes Northrop Frye, "has a comic sequel," and therefore "tragedy is really implicit or uncompleted comedy."[11] In one of those mysterious and challenging late works that take an almost mystical perspective on the human mind and its social embodiments, Freud speaks in detail about a particular game "played by a little boy of one and a half and invented by himself." The family had been impressed by how well the child adjusted to his mother's necessary absence; and yet

> this good little boy . . . had an occasional disturbing habit of taking any small objects he could get hold of and throwing them away from him into a corner, under the bed, and so on, so that hunting for his toys and picking them up was often quite a business. As he did this he gave vent to a loud long-drawn out 'o-o-o', accompanied by an expression of interest and satisfac-

tion. His mother and the writer of the present account were agreed in thinking that this was not a mere interjection but represented the German word 'fort' [gone]. I eventually realized that it was a game and that the only use he made of any of his toys was to play 'gone' with them. One day I made an observation which confirmed my view. The child had a wooden reel with a piece of string tied round it. It never occurred to him to pull it along the floor behind him, for instance, and play at its being a carriage. What he did was to hold the reel by the string and very skillfully throw it over the edge of his curtained cot, so that it disappeared into it, at the same time uttering his expressive 'o-o-o'. He then pulled the reel out of the cot again by the string and hailed its reappearance with a joyful 'da' [there]. This, then, was the complete game—disappearance and return.[12]

Freud is illustrating his concept of *mastery,* and suggesting that the human mind conquers painful experiences by obsessively repeating them in game and fantasy. And he reminds us that "the artistic play and artistic imitation carried out by adults, which, unlike children's, are aimed at an audience, do not spare the spectators (for instance in tragedy) the most painful experiences and can yet be felt by them as highly enjoyable."[13] Perhaps there is something on the individual psychic level that corresponds to those seasonal rituals of our collective past in which anthropologists have found a primal source of drama. Just as, in Freud's account, the child more frequently reenacted his mother's loss than her restoration, so tragedy too has always been considered more serious, more profound, more lofty than comedy. But remembering, for example, Dr. Johnson's well-known and frankly expressed abhorrence of the catastrophic final scene of *King Lear,* we may wish to add that most spectators find it more enjoyable when the painful experiences enacted on the stage prove to be merely a prelude to eventual happiness. In our heart of hearts, we prefer the completed game, the finished ritual, the celebration of spring rather than the reverent acknowledgment of winter; on the stage, we savor the obstacles to a desired goal insofar as we know they will be overcome, and enjoy the representation of despair particularly when we can expect that our losses will be restored, our differences reconciled. To paraphrase Dryden's famous comparison of his feelings for Jonson versus those for Shakespeare, most of us appreciate tragedy but love comedy.

The Renaissance critics seem also to have intuitively accepted the idea of comedy as a working through and final transcendence of tragedy. In the *Ars Poetica,* Horace made the fateful observation that all plays should have five acts (189), and his Renaissance interpreters tried their critical ingenuity at extreme length to explicate and justify this arbitrary scheme of dramatic structure. Christopher Landino, a Florentine scholar, published an edition of Horace ten years before the discovery of America and included a long note containing what became a generally accepted description of the five-act structure of a proper comedy. Following two acts of exposition, Landino prescribes that the third act should contain "the perturbation and the impediments and despair of the desired thing"; that act four should bring a "remedy for the impending evil"; and that act five should present, finally, "the desired outcome."[14] Donatus the Grammarian similarly observes, in one of his notes to Terence's *Andria,* that the exposition of the plot at the beginning of this play is left deliberately incomplete and misleading "that there may remain room for error."[15] Without errors there is no plot; without unhappy events, perturbations, complications, there can be no happy ending.

Even Freud's little boy had to endure his mother's absence in order to achieve an emotional mastery over it, and there is, in our emotional life, an enduring space for error that is, after all, our freedom. Perhaps it was our biological origins that imprinted this pattern on us, body and soul. When Freud speculates on the beginning of life on earth, he suggests that the earliest one-celled creature, the primal "living substance," contained a sort of inertia, a longing for inanimacy, and that only the very harshness of the world forced it, in instinctive opposition, "to make ever more complicated *détours* before reaching its aim of death."[16] Our ancestors suffered that they might live, and lived that we might suffer. Proverbial wisdom also speaks of the uses of adversity, and portrays suffering as the fruit of a deeply felt existence. The paradox of comedy is, then, the paradox of life. "At your age," Shaw's

Captain Shotover tells a young woman, "I looked for hardship, danger, horror and death . . . and my reward was, I had my life."[17] To be alive is itself a Saturnalia: a temporary reversal of inanimacy, a "holiday from death and night,"[18] a brief historical excursion between paradise lost and found. And comedy, in turn, reverses the conditions of mortality—in which time is our familiar enemy, not our ironic but certain friend; in which "Golden lads and girls all must, / As chimney sweepers, come to dust"; in which we live and love not happily ever after, but only till death do us part. In the theater the errors and perturbations of the characters are the play; in the world, the pain and process of living is life. Both there and here, despite unhappy endings, the show goes on.

Even at the furthest twilight of the human (and the comic) spirit, in those blank and indefinite spaces where Samuel Beckett systematically purges the drama of its redeeming coherence, there is still "Me to play." Some self, some face, some remnant of a voice, still shows itself, against all odds, theatrical. Beckett locates his comedy precisely in the no-man's-land between the play and the world. His characters and his audience face the same dilemma: *they* must get through their lives and *we* must get through the play. "What's happening, what's happening?" asks the main character of Beckett's masterpiece *Endgame*. The play's audiences may ask the same question—and receive the same answer: "Something is taking its course."[19] Stranded like us in the theatrical darkness, in an unspecified landscape of future time or despairing imagination, Hamm and Clove, Nagg and Neill manage to get through "this . . . this . . . thing," somehow making their dialogue a plot and themselves characters. "We're getting on," Hamm periodically reassures us, enduring as we do, his boredom and frustration, his ironic but inextinguishable self-interest.

Endgame is comedy stripped to the skeleton, to the merest blueprint of familiar comic devices and conventions. A father and a son, a master and a servant, share a series of passing conflicts which are, as it were, much ado about nothingness: a few last moments of gallows humor just this side of paralysis and annihilation:

HAMM. Sit on him!
CLOVE. I can't sit.
HAMM. True. And I can't stand.
CLOVE. So it is.
HAMM. Every man his speciality.
  (*Pause*)
  No phone calls?

This comedy goes beyond malice, beyond personality itself, to the purest incongruity of matter and spirit. There are few scenes in the history of comedy where comic derision turns so fiercely, excruciatingly, to recognition. Founded on the ironic identity between theater and life, *Endgame* returns again and again to that most ancient and characteristic of comic devices: the joke in which the actors "break" their characters and reveal frankly that the play is just a play:

CLOVE. (*He gets down, picks up the telescope, turns it on auditorium*)
  I see . . . a multitude . . . in transports . . . of joy.
  (*Pause*)
  That's what I call a magnifier.
  (*He lowers the telescope, turns toward Hamm*)
  Well, don't we laugh?
HAMM (*after reflection*). I don't.
CLOVE (*after reflection*). Nor I.

Here Beckett nods to the convention, but leaves his spectators separate and distant, their laughter disconnected from its object. In the comic tradition, by contrast, when a witty servant confides his schemes to the peanut gallery, or some ironist finally tires of the contrivances of the stage—

ORLANDO. Good day and happiness, dear Rosalind!
JACQUES. Nay then God buy you, and you talk in blank verse.
  (*As You Like It*, 4.1.30–31)

—we are *included* in the action: invited to share the comedy's magic and illusion as we will share symbolically in its concluding banquet. In Beckett, the effect of these jokes is entirely different:

CLOVE. What is there to keep me here?
HAMM. The dialogue.

Hamm and Clove admit they are part of a play *without* breaking character, because the dialogue is indeed the means and end of their shared existence. For these characters, the very last word in comic degradation, the play is, quite literally, the thing.

But even here, in this theater and this world, the show goes on: still tying the knot of complications—

CLOVE. (*He moves the telescope*)
    Nothing . . . nothing . . . good . . . good . . . nothing
    . . . goo—
    (*He starts, lowers the telescope, examines it, turns it again on the without. Pause.*)
    Bad luck to it!
HAMM. More complications! . . .
    Not an underplot, I trust.

—and still striving to achieve, if not a happy ending, then any kind of ending. The fragments of wit, occasional bursts of lyricism, and random literary echoes marooned among nonsense manage to get both the characters and us through this brief theatrical and historical moment before the rest is silence. Ironic comedy can go no further. The playwright is no longer godlike: he is more like the tailor in Nagg's joke:

NAGG. . . . "God damn you to hell, Sir, no it's indecent, there are limits! In six days, do you hear me, six days, God made the world. Yes, Sir, no less, Sir, than the WORLD! And you are not bloody well capable of making me a pair of trousers in three months?"
    (*Tailor's voice, scandalized*)
    "But my dear Sir, my dear Sir, look—
    (*disdainful gesture, disgustedly*)
    —at the world—
    (*pause*)
    and look—
    (*loving gesture, proudly*)
    —at my TROUSERS!"

Just so the playwright, holding up his play to the world, finds reason, one way or another, to be proud. Here, pausing at the butt end of our days and ways, comedy constricts our movement, and pinches in sensitive places: but it still fits, it still plays, and it still matters.

8 Medieval Mastery

We have been led through a series of poetic, proverbial, and critical insights to reexamine the sources of the comic impulse within the individual subconscious and our collective history. We can conclude, at least, that comedy is more than what Bergson called "a slight revolt on the surface of social life";[1] more than what Meredith described as a therapeutic fine-tuning of our manners and morals.

Comedy emerges from and reflects upon the society that produced it, but at the same time speaks to us as if it were outside of history, from the heart of one social context directly to our own. There is, as Ernst Bloch explains, a "cultural surplus" in the art produced by "the slave owning society of the ancient Greeks," or the "feudal-clerical" society of the Middle Ages, "something that moves above and beyond the ideology of a particular age. Only this 'plus' persists through the ages, once the social basis and ideology of an epoch have decayed; and remains as the substrate that will bear fruit and be a heritage for other times."[2] "Every jest," as Shaw was fond of reminding us, "is an earnest in the womb of time."[3] Turning back through history and the theatrical tradition, we are about to consider a few more instances of the comic spirit in which, as I see it, the "mirror" of what we are becomes a parable of what we can be.

"By help of God," wrote Menander, "evil, even as it comes to being, turns / To good."[4] For him, this was probably as much an ironic description of his own dramatic technique as a sincere vision of universal moral process. The Judeo-Christian tradition imposed this same comic structure on history, which it saw as a similar progress from separation to reconciliation. The Book of Job, for example, portrays the fundamental tragedy of humanity's relationship with God, but the story was finally canonized and edited into comedy, returning to its protagonist a greater share of wealth and fortune than he originally possessed. In Christian theology, the doctrine of the Fortunate Fall and the mystery of free will remind us of the paradox latent in comic drama. As in comedy there must be room for error, so in the world there must be room for injustice and doubt, for Fall and crucifixion; and as comic errors lead to happy endings, so the evil of the world produces

> . . . goodness infinite, goodness immense!
> That all this good of evil shall produce
> And evil turn to good;
> (*Paradise Lost,* 12.469–71)

At some ancient point of origin, long before Dante's poem inextricably linked the word *comedy* with the word *divine,* the religious and the comic visions may have mingled even more freely. Between the comic "faith" and the sacred Faith is a sort of punning likeness, an analogy itself comic that conceals, as Shaw might have put it, a hidden truth.

We do know that the longest running and most indisputably popular tradition of drama in our history was explicitly religious in both its origins and its content. Like classical tragedy and comedy, which are now assumed to represent a late, secular version of the seasonal rituals of our Indo-European ancestors, the so-called Corpus Christi cycles of the Middle Ages began as brief vernacular elaborations of the liturgy performed in church. These miniature dramas gradually moved to the church steps and from there

to the streets. Thus Western drama emerged from religious ritual
not once but twice, in both cases evolving as the secular equivalent
of a mystery, a festival celebrating the pride and faith of a united
community. In contrast to the fairly strict generic divisions of classical drama, the Corpus Christi plays embody that essential unity
of tragedy and comedy that modern criticism has rediscovered.
Most of the specific events that these plays portray are tragic: the
primal sin of Adam and Eve, the murder of Cain, the persecution
and crucifixion of Jesus. Yet the design of the whole cycle is
comic—portraying the reconciliation of all creation with its
benevolent creator, which follows the myriad perturbations of
mortal history. To a Christian, what will happen on earth is the
transformation of our human tragedy into divine comedy, and the
structure of the cycle embodies this religious and comic pattern. In
their totality, the cycles dramatize the universal potential for
salvation, and the inclusivity of this theological vision merges
with the leveling impulse of comedy in plays whose comic aspects
curiously deepen their genuine religious power. These plays portray characters "as they are" in real life, equal not just before God,
but also before the comic spirit.

In its social and economic conditions, furthermore, the Corpus
Christi drama seems to have overcome the paradoxes of dramatic
professionalism—the ironic contrasts between the interesting and
the interested artist—that we see in so many later comedians. In
these plays performed and paid for by craft guilds and supervised
by the civil corporation of each town, there was apparently no dis-
junction between the spiritual and financial value of entertainments that were, thus, "maintained by the people itself for its own
inexhaustible wonder and delight."[5] In the famous windows of
Chartres Cathedral, below each gloriously enthroned saint, ac-
companying each radiant scene of sacred history, there is also an
image of the specific craft whose guild assumed the cost of the
stained glass. A century or so later in England, the bourgeois
sponsors of the Corpus Christi plays seem to have assumed a similar identity between their own self-aggrandizement and their
munificent financial glorification of God. The intrinsic pleasures
of drama here compliment the bourgeois values and lives of its
sponsors and performers—who were, indeed, one and the same.

On the one hand, the amateur actors who performed these pageants could boast, as they do in the Chester bans, that they were
not "playeres of price."[6] On the other hand, the elaborate festivals of which the plays were the chief attraction probably also
paid off in terms of civic pride and prosperity. E. K. Chambers
records a sixteenth-century statement by "some old people who
had in their younger days been eye witnesses of these pageants,"
who claimed that "the confluence of people from farr and neare to
see that shew was extraordinarily great, and yielded no small advantage to this cittye."[7] As there was nothing sacrilegious about
a normal citizen assuming the dramatic role of Christ, so there
was nothing unethical about profiting from the dramatic reenactment of God's cosmic plan. In these festivals performed in honor
of the mystery of transubstantiation, there was no conflict between a play's spiritual significance and its material expense or
profit. In the Corpus Christi drama generally, according to F. M.
Salter, "we see the whole community at work in one great co-
operative enterprise dedicated to brisk business and the glory
of God."[8]

The most celebrated examples of the Corpus Christi drama are
the six plays that were apparently added to the so-called Townley
Cycle by an anonymous author usually referred to as the Wakefield Master. Without entering the scholarly debate about the
authorship of these plays and their chronological relation to the
rest of the cycle, we can still assume that the Wakefield group
is the achievement of a fairly sophisticated playwright who,
working within the framework of a preexisting cycle, chose to
dramatize some of the turning points of the cosmic comedy toward which, as he obviously believed, the manifold events of
human history were tending. Even outside the larger cycle, the
richness and variety of comic imagination in these separate plays
still embodies the Christian view of history: the raising of earth
to heaven, the transformation, as it were, of scatology to
eschatology.

In the *Mactacio Abel,* for example, the stark Latin title announces the fundamental tragedy of a play that still manages to be
funny, a play whose striking obscenity seems to embody the basic
comic incongruity between flesh and spirit, the human and the

divine. The Wakefield Master invites us to participate, through our laughter, in his theatrical reenactment of the primal act of violence by one man against another. At the beginning, Cain's servant assures us that his master is a socially respectable "good yeoman"; this killing comes from within us, out of the heart of the whole community. Still, the whole play does allow us to consider Cain as "worse" than ourselves in the Aristotelian sense (though the similarity must reflect some enduring aspect of comedy, not critical influence). The play ridicules Cain's perverse selfishness, his brutal violence and cowardice, and thus, in one aspect, the play unites an audience of presumed virtue in opposition to an offender against God and man alike. At the same time, the Wakefield Master elaborates the brief biblical account with comic detail that forces us to see in Cain something of our own reflection. All through the first part of the play, we've half forgotten this man is about to murder his brother. We're enjoying, as his original audience must have, his complaints about taxes and the boss, his apparent freedom from the constraints of authority. In this opening speech, the servant Garcio reminds us of other comical servants before and after him who greet their audiences both as character and actor. As he works the crowd, he also suggests a mocking identity between them and his master:

> All hayll, all hayll, both blithe and glad,
> For here com I, a mery lad!
> Be peasse youre dyn, my master bad,
> Or els the dwill you spede . . .
>
> Gedlyngys, I am a full grete wat.
> A good yeoman my master hat:
> Full well ye all hym ken.
> Begyn he with you for to stryfe,
> Certys, then mon ye neuer thryfe;
> But I trow, bi God on life,
> Som of you ar his men.
> (1–4; 14–23)[9]

We all do know Cain, as *character:* and we "welcom hym," as Garcio demands, in the theatrical sense at least. That the scoundrel should be an entertaining figure on the stage is an old and familiar paradox, realized in comic rogues like Falstaff or W. C. Fields. But here, a character who shall prove to be the inventor of treachery and murder bustles onto the stage preoccupied with an assortment of mundane concerns that must have been common irritations in his audience's own daily lives: stubborn oxen, an insolent servant and, finally, the pressing demands of God and his earthly agents for a portion of the hard-earned fruits of his labor.

In the ensuing dialogue, Cain asks why he should leave his business to make an offering to God, who has given him nothing but sorrow and from whom he never borrowed so much as a farthing. Because, says Abel, God has given you both your life and your living. Cain, however, is more concerned with the difficulties of the latter. In fact, he says, bringing it closer to the original audience's lives, my farthing has been in the priest's hand since the last time I made an offering. This scene portrays a collision between an earthly and a spiritual perspective, and we verify with laughter our inevitable, momentary sympathy with the former. The Wakefield Master has allowed Cain to stand as if in the place of the *eiron*, deflating an apparent imposter's pretense of knowledge. So the whole scene forms a kind of divine Saturnalia, inverting the universal relations of virtue and authority. The play continues with a Punch-and-Judy routine in which Cain tries ludicrously to shortchange an all-seeing deity. Here, we are laughing at two different comic targets and their contrast: Abel's slow-witted reluctance to acknowledge his brother's evil and Cain's outrageous scatological insults hurled to the heavens.

> ABELL. Came, of God me thynke thou has no drede.
> CAME. Now and he gets more, the dwill me spede!—
>   As much as oone reepe—
>   For that cam hym full light chepe;
>   Not as mekill, grete ne small,
>   As he myght wipe his ars withall.
> (233–38)

We enjoy both Cain's blasphemy and his powerlessness against divine authority. This kind of comedy, coming so perilously close

to genuine sacrilege, could only have been the product of an un-
shakably genuine faith.

Moreover, these scenes depicting Cain's comical attempts to
deny God's power over him actually lead us to a particular way of
viewing the tragic event that gives the play its title. In the Bible,
neither Cain nor Abel questions God's existence or power; Cain is
simply jealous that their common master has favored Abel's offering over his own, and his act, therefore, is one of personal jealousy
and violence against the preferred brother. In the Wakefield version, by subtle contrast, Cain is infuriated specifically because
God's rejection of his offering vindicates Abel's point of view in
their comical debate, so the murder itself becomes a perverse
acknowledgment of God's authority. Cain in effect proclaims to
the audience the value of divine favor by his rage over losing that
favor. The death of Abel tips the comic scale against Cain: choked
with smoke from his unsuccessful offering, he becomes the butt of
God's joke (indeed he is hoist with his own petard, almost literally). Then, having destroyed his former straight man, he must
finish the play ridiculed by Garcio's mocking asides to the audience. Before our eyes, the ironist is transformed into an imposter:
the likable skeptic of the earlier part of the play now hides beneath
God's reflected glory, and it is Garcio who deflates him with a
down-to-earth cynicism. When Cain tries to rejoin the repartee,
all that remains of his former colorful language is an uncomfortable and unintentional irony:

> For bot it were Abell, my brothere,
> Yit knew I neuer thy make.
> (442–43)

The Wakefield Master repeats this joke to exactly opposite effect
in his Noah play, where, a bare hundred or so lines after God has
acknowledged the virtue of Noah and his wife (103–8), Noah
exclaims angrily to his audience:

> In fayth, I hold non slyke
> In all medill-erd.
> (233–34)

In this moment, it is as if God gives Noah a greater comic power than Noah knows: for the audience already understands that there *is* none like his wife in all the earth. An insult born of momentary exasperation becomes an ironic compliment. Cain's act of irreparable evil, by contrast, dries up the force of his comic skill, leaving only the irony of Garcio's bitterly parodic concluding benediction:

> Now old and yong, or that ye weynd,
> The same blissyng withoutten end,
> All sam then shall ye haue,
> That God of heuen my master has giffen.
> (444–47)

We have seen some happy endings announce themselves as gifts of art, suggesting that the audience remember *this is not the way it should or would have been.* But this play ends on a note of humorously expressed despair—an inverted blessing that invites the audience to cynical laughter but that also reminds them *this is not the way it had to be.* Cain's loss is our gain.

Thus the Wakefield Master's vision of history is direct and causal, not ironic; or if so, only with the cosmic irony that Cain's misfortune leads, by example, to the true "blissyng withoutten end" still available to all. Where Euripides' Helen enacts a comic plot whose fortunate resolution seems disproportionate to its historical context, Cain earns his own fate both theologically and theatrically. The dramatic texture of the Wakefield plays mirrors the paradox of free will: for as each human being's fate is preordained and yet freely willed, so the divine plan of the whole Corpus Christi cycle is embodied and enacted by "realistic" characters enmeshed in their own individual destinies as well as in the larger structure of events. Helenic drama was, from the first, preeminently concerned with the individual, yet in its late tragicomic or comic forms it increasingly portrayed characters caught within a dramatic structure in which chance mirrors and confirms choice, in which their own "wicked deeds," as Menander put it, are rectified by "haphazard luck."[10] The medieval drama went in the reverse direction, moving from a "vertical" concern with the unique emblems and actors of a few significant events of divine history, to a "horizontal" image of ordinary human beings living their lives in and around the moment of revelation. After all, the whole point of the revelations is their effect on those ordinary lives. The theological vision apparently participated in the development of a "realistic" drama, and that drama in turn embodies the manifestation of God's will by and in human history.

The Wakefield Master's finest experiments with this rediscovered comic realism, this unique synthesis of comedy and tragedy, are the First and Second Shepherds' plays. Here alone among the surviving Corpus Christi plays are two versions of the same subject which, as we can conclude from textual evidence alone, were written by the same playwright, and which allow us to see the development of that playwright's dramatic imagination. The essential similarity of the two plays makes it unlikely that both would have been performed as part of the same yearly festival. Rather, the Second Shepherd's Play seems to be a revision and elaboration of an earlier effort in which the random but emblematical clowning of the first play becomes a fully realized dramatic plot. The second version is unique among all the cycle plays, presenting us with a totally separate human drama which unfolds on its own terms even as it reflects thematically and iconographically on the play's "real" subject, the birth of Christ. Going from the First to the Second Shepherd's Play, we witness the Wakefield Master's growing awareness of the uses of comedy, but in both we can see an evocative relationship between the individual and the collective destinies, between the characters' personal human comedies and the grander divine comedy in which the characters also play their part.

Certainly these two plays seem mysteriously to echo or foreshadow comedies from other ages that can have neither influenced nor been influenced by them. Both plays concern a group of lower-class characters who come into conflict with each other and who then, for no apparent reason, become witnesses of the most significant event of earthly history. As Dante might have commented, the beginnings of both plays are miserable, while the endings are fortunate and joyful. The characters are caught between self-interest and an interest in the universe. Their progress on what is, unbeknownst to them, the most important day of their lives, reflects both the classical notion of comedy and the archetypal comic contrast between matter and spirit. Here you are, these plays suggest, thrown into the middle of a divine plan, and all you can think about is your next meal. In the second play, it is impossible to miss how Mak's theft of real lamb, absurdly disguised as a newborn baby, mirrors the birth of the Lamb of God. This obvious parallelism, mocking and exalting the human comedy, helps make the play the most celebrated example of medieval drama—one that even clings to a narrow place in the modern theatrical repertoire, remaining familiar to many from church carnivals and Christmas pageants.

But the First Shepherd's Play, less discussed and probably superseded even on the medieval stage, is perhaps an even more subtle example of this comic typology. This play begins with a shepherd's complaining to us about the hardships of life for a man who has lost his living. His sheep have all died from disease, he explains, but by his wit, and with God's grace, he intends to start over,

> And yit may I multiple
> For all this hard case.
> (44–45)

Outside the context and poetic texture, the shepherd may remind us of Middleton's Witt-good in *A Trick to Catch the Old One,* or of other characters whose lack of money initiates the action in many other comedies. Except that, exactly where we might expect an appeal to good fortune, the shepherd instead states merely that "if hap will grynde" (if Chance afflicts me), then "god from his heven / Send grace!" In this play, Chance is an obstacle, not an ally. The playwright is once again in a godlike position, because he controls the story and its ending, but this play will bring no final redoubling of the protagonist's flock and herds. Now another shepherd comes on stage to complain about a certain upstart servant who "will make it as prowde a lord as he were." With his head in the clouds, his loud voice and grim bearing, says the shepherd, you can hardly tell the master from the man. (A very different comic writer four centuries later would have called the fellow a "snob.")[11] This apparently irrelevant and anachronistic social detail points thematically to the later revelation of heaven's genuine hierarchies. For at the end of the play, in a kind of transcendent Saturnalia, the lowly shepherds are vouchsafed the vision of Christ's birth, which, as they are quick to remind us, many prophets "desyrd veralee" (441).

The opening speeches are followed, however, by scenes of comic horseplay whose humorous effect relies at least partly on a keen awareness of class distinctions. These scenes allow us to laugh *at* characters who are both socially and personally worse than their presumed audience. Whatever each spectator's social rank may be, the play forces him or her to take a shifting and complex view of its characters. For example, these shepherds whose poverty has won our initial sympathy proceed to fight over the grazing rights of what we already know to be their nonexistent sheep:

> 1 PASTOR. . . . I say give the shepe space.
> 2 PASTOR. Syr, a letter of your grace!

Standing on their own petty and imaginary dignity, threatening violence over a phantom object, the shepherds may even remind us of Euripides' fantastic retelling of the Trojan War—and the scene seems to be intended, similarly, as a parable of the tragic (and comic) uselessness of conflict. After the entrance of a third shepherd, more clowning, and mutual insults, all three sit down to eat and drink, only to pull from their pouches what seems to be an equally imaginary supply of noblemen's delicacies, "chekyne endorde, pork, partry to roys, / A tart for a lorde" (234–35). The whole scene, filled with an incongruous mixture of rustic, religious, courtly, legal, and obscene language, is a deliberately contradictory image of ridiculous social pretense and genuine human community. We hear the triumphant and shameless folk laughter of which Mikhail Bakhtin speaks, the bawdy and corporeal images that celebrate "the people's unofficial truth," and we also witness that social exorcism of affectations and institutional jargon that much later theorists would see as the only true comic function. All in all, this scene conveys a multiple perspective on contemporary society which finally merges into a utopian affirmation. "I fare full ill / At your manger," the third shepherd complains, and his words remind us of another manger where, as we shall see at the end of the play, he will fare better than at this table. The first shepherd's mock legalisms, similarly, point our attention toward the birth of that King before whose Justice there are no professionals. Just afterwards, the second shepherd drains the cup of wine that all three had been sharing:

> 2 PASTOR. I shrew the handys it drogh!
>   Ye be both knafys.
> 1 PASTOR. Nay, we knaues all; thus thynk we best,
>   So, syr, shuld ye call.

The first shepherd's pun, at once humorous and solemn, plays on the two contemporary meanings of the word *knafe*—either a "rogue" or "knave" in the modern sense, or "a person of humble birth." These men are "knaues all" in both senses, perhaps. Yet the ultimate purport of this joke both embodies and transcends the critical ambiguity about the social versus moral "lowness" of comic characters. Critics of a later age would, as we have considered, try to make the comic spirit a snob, as if trying against all odds and reason to confirm that society's hierarchies do reflect a human being's genuine "quality." Here, the same comedy that mocks its lower-class characters also exalts them; the same comedy that depends on class distinctions no less than will the "genteel" comedies of centuries later, unlike those later plays, also denies such distinctions. In this wonderful scene, the comedy of aggression and superiority becomes the comedy of fellowship. The audience has not even finished laughing at the actors on this stage when the shepherds they represent, poor men themselves, decide to resolve their quarrel by giving their imaginary luxuries away to "hungre begers, frerys!"[12] On this note of humorous and unsentimental charity, the angelic messenger descends.

For the Wakefield Master, in other words, the Holy Spirit and the comic spirit are finally the same. The sacred presence that speaks from above or descends in the middle of the earthly drama is both the human actor we expect and the God who has expectations of us. The playwright's theatrical self-consciousness leaves us with reverence rather than cynicism, and our perception of the inevitable ironies of dramatic performance somehow leads us to a larger mystery. This is why Cain, hearing the divine admonition thundering down to his human ears, can make us laugh by asking

> Whi, who is that hob over the wall?
> We! who was that that piped so small?
> (*Mactacio Abel*, 297–98)

This is funny because the audience knows—as the *character* Cain should not—that the voice did come from an actor on a platform speaking with histrionic but unamplified authority. Like Plautus and so many other comic playwrights, the Wakefield Master invites us to catch sight of ourselves as spectators at a play, but here it is as though Cain turns away from truth when he ridicules the dramatic illusion, and turns away from God when he denies the human actor as God. It is this high seriousness about what Molière called the strange business of making people laugh, that gives these medieval plays their special power. Cain is laughing uncomfortably at a reality that is impinging on his denial of it; we are laughing at the spectacular power and comic inadequacy of dramatic impersonation. The Wakefield Master causes his audience to suspend their disbelief to reaffirm their belief. At the beginning of the First Shepherd's Play, we may remember, the shepherd had resolved to "cast the warld in seven" (39), hazarding his remaining possessions in a last attempt to regain his lost flock. At the end, Mary promises "good endyng" to him and his fellows in the name of the Lord who "sett all on seven," who made the universe in seven days (485–94). Creation too is a comedy of loss and restoration. The play never quite lets us know how things will work out for its comical shepherds. But we take their happy ending on faith.

9 Mayakovsky's Mystery

The medieval festivals of sacred comedy lasted almost to Shakespeare's day before they were silenced by puritan opposition, but by that time they had already contributed their realistic texture and versatile conception of theatrical space to the fruitful synthesis of Renaissance drama. In a wider sense too, the "cultural surplus" of which Bloch speaks also survived, to blossom again in the most incongruous of new settings, and to realize once more a utopian vision of human community and meaningful history. Appropriately enough, the modern half of our account also begins with a kind of ritual, a performance that was part of a public festival and that defined itself both by its similarity and its difference from the religious drama of the past. In 1918, a young Russian poet and playwright sent an outline of a theatrical entertainment to something called the Central Committee for the Organization of the October Celebrations, envisioning a comic spectacle to celebrate the year-old Russian Revolution. His only previous play, an extreme example of romantic self-expression called *Vladimir Mayakovsky: A Tragedy,* sometimes approached the ludicrous but was otherwise the artistic opposite of this new proposal. Where Mayakovsky's former play was intensely private, this one

would be explicitly public; where the former had tried to inflict that "Slap at Public Taste" that he and three fellow "futurist" writers had promised in their Manifesto of 1912, this one would adapt a deliberately naive and direct dramatic style. Mayakovsky's *Tragedy*, as its title suggests, points vaguely in the direction of classical Greece, and the second act opens with the poet-hero wearing "a toga and laurel wreath," burdened with the praises of an uncomprehending multitude.[1] With the revolution, however, Mayakovsky's avant-garde pretense seems to merge with a deeper belief in the future and its potential, and he turns to the very different model of a medieval religious play. Calling his new work *Mystery-Bouffe*, Mayakovsky announces himself as a new voice in the comic tradition. The finished work would provide the inexperienced actors who would sponsor and perform the modern pageant with a secular equivalent of the sacred comedy of the bourgeois past.

Such, at least, seems to have been his intention. *Mystery-Bouffe* is a unique and eccentric play that is not easy to judge or summarize. It has little in common with Mayakovsky's own work either before or after it and even less with the so-called socialist realism of the next generation of Soviet writers. Yet Mayakovsky's use of the medieval model, in the terms of our argument, has a striking appropriateness. The parody and transformation of medieval religious imagery mirrors the Marxist vision of history, in which socialism emerges from the wealth and resources of capitalism, and in which a more glorious present is to be built with the tools of the past. The comic structure of the Corpus Christi drama derives from and embodies the paradoxical theology of human freedom, and Mayakovsky finds a parallel between that same comic structure and the Marxist paradox that joins freedom and determinism in a dialectical unity. The belief in an all-knowing God does not abrogate a Christian's personal moral responsibility, and in an analogous manner, Marxism "called upon human beings for a supreme deed of free will, that of intervening in their history with a revolutionary act and creating their own society. But it did so with a necessitarian vocabulary, so that the working class in its highest moment of freedom was fulfilling historical necessity."[2] The characters of Marxist history, as of

Christian history, play their parts in a universal comedy that constantly moves toward its inevitable and expected happy ending. As in the play there must be room for error and conflict, so in the world there must be room for capitalism and the class struggle it engenders. Marx called, in effect, for an end to the drama of historical conflict, looking toward that final reconciliation of all humanity with itself when "in place of the old bourgeois society, with its classes and class antagonisms, we shall have an association in which the free development of each is the condition for the free development of all."[3] Thus Mayakovsky, like the Wakefield Master, contrasts the farce of specific events with the grandeur of the total story. Like the medieval drama on which it is based, *Mystery-Bouffe* takes the universe for a stage and enacts the whole history of the world with the conventional characters of the comic tradition. This unique modern play portrays, as it were, the comic sequel to the world's historical tragedy.

As with the Corpus Christi drama, this play would not be performed by professionals. An advertisement in the Petrograd papers announced the production of Mayakovsky's revolutionary extravaganza and appealed as much to the political commitment of potential actors as to their dramatic skill or experience:

> Comrade actors! It is your duty to celebrate the great day of the revolution with a revolutionary show. You should perform *Mystery-Bouffe*—the heroic, epic and satiric picture of our era. . . . Let all come on Sunday, October 13 to the concert hall. . . . Time is precious![4]

In retrospect, there is something at once moving and comic about this passage—which assumes a paradoxical identity between duty and entertainment and effortlessly pairs the word *revolution* with the word *show*. The students and scattered professionals who formed the original cast felt a similar mixture of cynicism and admiration. As one of them recounts, the play

> at first, made us laugh and sometimes joke. None of us understood anything at all. . . . Mayakovsky worked with us like a dog, explaining the meaning and reading the text over and over again. . . . The day suddenly came—it was, I think, the

tenth or eleventh rehearsal—when we felt not only that we understood what the play was all about but that we liked it and were won over by it as well. We came to like the verse. We knew not only our own parts but whole fragments, scenes and monologues by heart. . . . We began to quote from *Mystery* in our conversations.[5]

The process of creating this play took the actors from skeptical laughter to the comedy of understanding and affection. At the first performance, despite the mixed reactions that the play elicited from its spectators, "we, the participants," as our witness recounts, "felt a great satisfaction. The audacity and novelty of all this enchanted us." As must have been the case during the Corpus Christi festivals, the play affirmed a sense of community as much in its literal conditions as in what it expressed. The performers were actors of the revolution in both senses. "The most interesting thing about *Mystery-Bouffe*," argued a contemporary reviewer, "is that Mayakovsky . . . the first among futurist poets, has clearly said 'we.' At that moment he ceased to be a romantic and became a classic."[6]

It is not necessary to say very much about the specific "plot" of this sprawling and unconventional play—in which, after all, the performance is the mirror, rather than vice versa. When a new flood destroys the world, a group of working people, the "Unclean," escapes in an ark and, while fighting the treachery and deceptions of the "Clean," travels through Hell, Purgatory, and Heaven, and finally finds the true paradise reborn on earth. Along the way, there are bits of slapstick, topical satire, and occasional bursts of lyricism. In his treatment of this incongruous, even ludicrous subject matter, Mayakovsky addresses and finally transcends the paradox of dramatic realism, embodying in theatrical action that Marxist aspiration to transform the minds of humanity by transforming their social reality. In his prologue to the revised version of 1921, Mayakovsky takes a slap, not at the public taste but at Chekhov and the realistic tradition of theater. In traditional drama, he complains, the stage is "a keyhole without a key," and all you can see is Uncle Vanya and Auntie Manya chattering on a sofa:

We too, will show you life that's real—
very!
But life transformed by the theatre into a spectacle most
    extraordinary!

To paraphrase Marx's most famous dictum, previous playwrights
have only *represented* the world; the point, however, is to *change*
it. Here, we can see how Mayakovsky's avant-garde impulse to
desecrate the art of the past merges with a quasi-classical attempt
to teach and delight; while his naive joy in the spectacle of theater
merges with a revolutionary commitment to transform history.

In the body of the play, similarly, Mayakovsky tries to exploit
the intrinsic irony of acting a part to express a sense of human
potential. His satire mocks things as they are, while his plot
directs us to things as they can be, a double-edged theatrical effect
that carried over to his directorial style. From the actors playing
the bourgeois politicians and intellectuals of the Clean, another
contemporary observer recalls that Mayakovsky "was willing to
tolerate exaggerated parody, including the somewhat coarse elements of satiric buffoonery and popular farce."[7] For these characters, there would be familiar scenes of imaginary conflict and ludicrous pretense—as in the beginning, when Lloyd George and
Clemenceau quarrel like children over the last dry bit of land in
a world engulfed by water:

> LLOYD GEORGE. My flag is planted.
>   I'm undisputed master in this snowy clime.
> CLEMENCEAU. I beg to differ!
>   My flag was set up first.
>   This colony is mine.
> LLOYD GEORGE (*laying out some trading goods*).
>   No, it's not. It's mine.
>   I'm already trading, see?
> CLEMENCEAU (*getting angry*).
>   Oh no! It belongs to me.
>   Go look for another place.
> LLOYD GEORGE (*furious*).
>   What?
>   You can go to hell!

This is not what most critics would consider a complex or subtle kind of drama, but it is a fascinating effort to return to the emblematic, simplified drama of an earlier age, in which the most serious ideas could stir an audience to triumphant and comprehending laughter.

Thus in this play the bourgeoisie is again a comic butt, but this time the mockery comes from the other side of the social spectrum. *Mystery-Bouffe* is also, as Mayakovsky had advertised, a "heroic" work, and, from the actors who played the Unclean, he demanded "strong will, heroic pathos, and grandeur." Later in the play, for example, the Unclean storm Hell only to find its horrors mere pretense, milder than the infernal landscape of the human past. "What have you got?" the blacksmith asks the devil,

> A whiff of sulfur, that's all!
> On earth, when they use poison gas,
> whole regiments fall
> like clipped grass,
> and the plain turns gray with the coats of the dead.

This Chaplinesque mixture of broad farce and pathos is the exact opposite of the socialist realism which a postrevolutionary Soviet state demanded of its artistic servants. Banishing experimentation and "obscurity," addicted to happy endings unearned by character or plot, the school of socialist realism "while outwardly upholding the representational-reflection theory of art as their model, secretly practice the enforcement of ideological deception, of utopian construct."[8] In this "poster and slogan style" of art,[9] a strict adherence to an official line of truth turns an apparent realism into the crudest sort of fantasy. But in *Mystery-Bouffe,* for a brief theatrical moment, the work day was the holiday, the social rebels were the society, and the truest poetry was truly the most feigning. Mayakovsky embodies, rather than represents, a vision and a reality of social possibility.

Indeed, in this play the dei ex machina who announce the happy ending are literal machines. At the end, the fruits of the earth, and the tools made by and for human hands stream from the earthly city in a personified allegorical procession, imploring forgiveness from the workers they formerly enslaved. Thus the play ends, rather than begins, with the Saturnalian image of social reversal, announcing itself as possibility instead of pretense. In its final lines, the full union of cynicism and optimism is also the union of theatrical illusion and reality:

> All shout Hurrah!
> Hurrah for everything!
> Today,
> these are only stage-prop doors,
> but tomorrow, reality will replace
> this theatrical trash.
> We know this.
> We believe in it.
> Up here, spectators!
> Up here, artist!
> Poet!
> Director!
> (*All the spectators mount the stage*)

With this, perhaps the most extraordinary stage direction in the history of drama, reaching out to enfold the whole community of author, actors, and audience, Mayakovsky touches something profound in the nature of comedy itself, a familiar note of fellowship that bridges the centuries of the comic tradition even as it points toward a splendidly real future. We are instructed, with familiar cynicism, to disbelieve in the "theatrical trash" of the present performance. But we are also allowed to stand at the threshold of a new world that the scenery doors prefigure. Comic plays have always pretended to invite us to the banquet, to take hands in the concluding dance; but here, Mayakovsky asks us literally to ascend the stage, in a happy ending that tries to become what it has enacted.

Some of the play's original spectators were unimpressed, labeling the play "coarse" and "vulgar."[10] A modern American student of Mayakovsky's work, seeing *Mystery-Bouffe* as a period piece and not much more, concludes simply that "there may be some still left whose faith is so naive that they would find Mayakovsky's 'mystery play' a moving experience."[11] As the sophisticated ironies of a Machiavelli or a Middleton left us at the impasse of our own personal morality, so Mayakovsky's deliberate naïveté leaves us with our own faith. Perhaps the critic's retrospective cynicism is only an ironic measure of the play's own insistent optimism. Perhaps the "universal character" of transcendent comedy is "impossible without a share of vulgarity."[12] I make no apologies for whatever it is that still moves me in *Mystery-Bouffe,* and argue, by extension, that as all disillusion is the product of experience, so all faith is finally innocent, a naïveté that "confounds the pretence of wisdom."[13] Such innocence lies at the heart of Mayakovsky's play and its medieval antecedents, making possible a vision of comic benevolence uncontradicted by observation, a mirror of reality uncontaminated by cynicism.

10   The Shavian Solution

The spirit, structure, or experience we call comedy is more than the institution that brings it into life. Comedy is mere entertainment and illusion, but somewhere in its long history it began to be used, not always wittingly, for some very different kinds of moral and thematic purpose. We have been seeing the connections between the purpose and the illusion; between each author's ideological goals, conscious or unconscious, and his peculiar kind of self-consciousness. As the comic spirit enacted itself in different ages, sometimes life was just a play and sometimes the play was the thing; and Terence's "nothing human is foreign to me" alternates with "you can't cheat an honest man." The ironic comedies of the second section declare themselves to be "just plays" with a deliberately contrived use of comic conventions: placing recognizably corrupt, hypocritical, or affected characters within a clockwork plot whose perfection mocks their imperfection. The rarer transcendent comedy declares itself to be "just a play" by pointing toward that historical possibility of which the dramatic happy ending is a type. Thus a popular entertainment that sometimes indulges us with malice and superiority, parading our most trivial

emotions to the public view, can also point us beyond our individual concerns toward a common future.

With the medieval and modern comedies of history and faith, we essentially complete what has been our account of the furthest tendencies of the comic spirit. But I want to consider one more playwright who still retains a narrow hold on the contemporary stage, and who remains, in the established theater, probably our only source of that transcendent laughter that recalls us to comedy's origins and realizes its potential. George Bernard Shaw makes an appropriate conclusion, because in his life and works, as in the characteristic voice and attitude that his very name suggests, we find a fulfillment and reinterpretation of the comic tradition. For example: when he was once asked if he believed in the Immaculate Conception, he merely expressed his belief that all conceptions are immaculate. The particular effect of this joke shows what happens when comedy unites itself with faith—and how the familiar incongruity between a mundane and a cosmic perspective can also take us through irony to the truth behind it. Shaw's joke mocks the formal doctrine even as it concedes the mystic fact, seeing a double meaning in both terms of the comic equation. For "conceive . . . is the word," as the serpent in *Back to Methusaleh* puts it, "that means both the beginning in imagination and the end in creation."[1] The particular Shavian kind of comedy—one part wit and one part humor (as Thackeray might have put it), critical, even savage, but reassuringly brilliant—embodies what I have called the paradox of comedy and reaches to a synthesis of comedy's conflicting impulses.

Indeed, the comic rhythm of denial and affirmation is also the rhythm of Shaw's career. His writings separate naturally into the play and the preface, the imagined and the real; the comedies on which his major reputation depends are themselves strange mixtures of metaphysical daring and traditional entertainment, philosophic realism and the frankest of theatrical contrivance. Looking back to the ironic comedians who defined his tradition, Shaw concludes that "comedy, as a destructive, derisory, critical, negative art, kept the theater open when sublime tragedy perished," but that "ever since Shakespeare, playwrights have been struggling with their lack of positive religion. Many of them were forced to become mere panders and sensation mongers because, though they had higher ambitions, they could find no better subject matter."[2] As for Shaw's own positive religion, it is probably true that "any philosophy student could make mincemeat of Creative Evolution as a logically constructed system."[3] Probably some of Shaw's myriad economic, political, biological, and "meta-biological" ideas would seem indefensible outside the splendid rhetoric with which he clothed them. But the plays really communicate not a creed, but a simple prescription for action; not a religion, but a faith in and responsibility toward the future. In this, despite doctrinal and political differences, he betrays a spiritual kinship to the Wakefield Master and to Mayakovsky, sharing their comic vision of comprehensible history. For Shaw too, a belief in the future turned the comic convention of optimism into a vision of the possible.

Not that he was above a bit of sensation mongering himself. Like the playwrights of the previous section, Shaw confronts us as both pander and preacher, allowing the contradictions of his public image to mirror the contradictions of comedy. Thus the short-tempered and irascible GBS whom the British public came to know so well, the self-advertiser arrogantly declaring his superiority to Shakespeare, was in a different sense the most humble of artists who found "the true joy in life" in "being used for a purpose" greater than himself, and who swore that his plays came "straight from the Life Force."[4] He would remind us often that he wrote plays to make money, and he exacted his full royalties with the unsentimental explanation that they were only his due. He would argue that "all artists make their living as pleasure merchants," and he tells us frankly that when he was once accosted by "a lady of the pavement," he found himself "touched by the similarity of our trades."[5] But this amiable cynic, in a different mood, would contrast the "Ephemeral Thrones" of the secular world with the Platonic reality of "the Eternal Theatre," and, insisting that his conscience was "the genuine pulpit article," would affirm that he labored in the drama not for art's sake but for our sake.[6] Thus the squire of Ayot St. Lawrence was really the witty servant of the Life Force; thus the merchant of illusions, the self-interested author of commercial potboilers, was in his own view no more

personally important than the medium who transcribes the mystic
utterances of a transcendent voice. The faith he shared with us
was itself profoundly comic:

> There is an indescribable levity—not triviality, mind, but
> levity—something sprite-like about the final truth of a matter;
> and this exquisitive levity communicates itself to the style of
> a writer who will face the labour of digging down to it. It is the
> half-truth which is congruous, heavy, serious and suggestive of
> a middle-aged or elderly philosopher. The whole truth is often
> the first thing that comes into the head of a fool or a child; and
> when a wise man forces his way to it through the many strata of
> his sophistications, its wanton, perverse air reassures him in-
> stead of frightening him.[7]

Here is a version of Meredith's comic spirit that has turned its
back on the sophistications of the drawing room. It is this sprite-
like creature of reassuring folly who hovers over Shaw's articulate
comic characters, who presides over that personal Saturnalia in
which the playwright, reversing the high seriousness of his moral
convictions, assumed the cap and bells that he might speak the
truth. "In order to get a hearing," Shaw explains in his most
famous self-advertisement, "it was necessary for me to attain the
footing of a privileged lunatic, with the license of a jester." But
where the Saturnalian comedy of the past indulges us with entertaining images of freedom and equality only to reassure us at the
end that the whole thing was just a joke, Shaw makes us laugh and
then reveals "the real joke is that I am in earnest."[8]

Painted, sculpted, and photographed as much as any man of
our century, Shaw made us remember not just his writings but
also his face, with savage indignation hiding beneath the painted
grin of the classical comic mask. Even before he had written his
first play, Shaw had learned how to spellbind an audience with
iconoclastic wit, how to turn his rage and sorrow into epigraphs.
By the masterpieces of his middle period, Shaw has discovered
within the structure of comic plots a model for his particular
vision of historical and metabiological process. Some of his early
efforts in the comedy of ideas adapt a more negative method. In
Widowers' Houses, for example, Shaw simply inverts the tradi-

tional comic plot, making the play into an extreme example of the ironic comic mode. The characters are hypocritical, affected, and finally ridiculous, like most of the comic characters we know; but they are also criminally negligent (to paraphrase Aristotle's description of the comic mask) in a manner that does imply pain. The plot resolves itself with a marriage and closes with a feast, but the attachment of Blanche Sartorius and Harry Trench merely allows the other characters to consummate a business deal. The projected wedding, in fact, is also a vehicle for an even less honorable form of real-estate exploitation than the slum landlordism that will continue to support the happy couple. Thus the most ancient and familiar of comic motifs becomes, in this play, an emblem of prevailing corruption instead of reconciliation—and this corruption, as we metaphorically join in the wedding banquet, is ours as well. As one critic puts it, this comic ending makes its spectators "shrink from contact with one another."[9] The on-stage image of familial joy directs our thoughts to a larger off-stage misery, its cause and effect.

By the time of *Man and Superman,* some ten years later, Shaw has perfected a dramatic method at once more complex and more truly comic. This play, like what Don Juan will call the "clock-maker's pendulum" of evolutionary process, seems to swing back and forth between the two poles of the comic dialectic. In its characters and situations, *Man and Superman* echoes traditional comic images in a manner that both confirms and questions their original significance. "Enry" Straker, for example, is a latter-day version of the Plautine witty slave whose relationship to his type is doubly ironic. His ancestor on the comic stage was usually a sort of "poet" of ingenious mischief, a comic master-of-ceremonies whose chicanery moves the plot and fulfills the spectators' vicarious desires. As we have seen, this embodiment of freedom and irrepressible vitality is allowed to deceive and victimize his master on the stage only to reaffirm the inviolable authority of that master in real life. But Straker's superiority to his "master," John Tanner, is mundane, specific, and entirely "realistic." As chauffeur, he is a symbol and a representative not of wit but of know-how, not of misrule but of technological responsibility. Shaw has distorted the Saturnalian situation in a strangely prophetic manner: the real joke is that the modern world makes us slaves of our own life-enhancing machines and the specialized knowledge required to run them. Traditional comedy, reversing social relations on the stage, lets the audiences have it both ways, indulging their enjoyment of unofficial truths but also their conservative commitment to society as it is. Shaw's portrayal of this modern servant, however, lets us have it neither way. For no sooner have we enjoyed Straker as *eiron*, deflating bourgeois pretense—

> OCTAVIUS. I believe most intensely in the dignity of labor.
> STRAKER (*unimpressed*). Thats because you never done any, Mr. Robinson.

—than Straker proceeds, as Tanner puts it, to act "just like a miserable gentleman," betraying his own slavery to class distinctions and outmoded morality. Thus Shaw directs our attention to the hidden conservatism of the convention by showing how, in real life, servitude creates a reactionary, not a radical class consciousness. At the same time, Shaw allows Straker to embody a vision more truly subversive than any classical slave's mere insolence and mischief by making him an "anticipation of the efficient engineering class which will . . . finally sweep the jabberers out of the way of civilization."[10]

In the subplot involving Violet and Hector Malone, similarly, Shaw seems at first to have simply reversed the conventional comic situation of *The Clandestine Marriage* (as David Garrick titled one version of it). In this case, the rich father's inverted snobbery demands a bourgeois "social profit" from his son's marriage, and thus he objects to the bride and groom's being of equal, not unequal, social rank. But later, when Hector Malone, Sr., capitulates to Violet's unsentimental determination and will, without any fortuitous revelations of identity or inheritance, we realize that Shaw is, once again, inviting us to reconsider the meaning of the ancient convention. Throughout the comic tradition, Shaw seems to be saying, the innumerable lovers who evade parental opposition were not just affirming what Terence had already described as a generation gap.[11] The real comic conflict, Shaw suggests, was not between youth and age, but between the Life Force and all the social constraints that bind or limit it.

Comedy and its audiences always side with the young because their romantic schemes and intrigues, however ridiculous, embody life's incessant struggle to perpetuate itself. The theatrical devices of coincidence and recognition were mere contrivances of the playwright to meet the parents' objections and thus resolve the plot; so too, as Tanner and Shaw would see it, is marriage itself a mere contrivance of the Life Force to insure a sufficient number of children and adequate care for them. Tanner's *Revolutionist's Handbook* argues that marriage may no longer be a requirement in human reproduction, and accordingly, Shaw resolves Violet's difficulties without recourse to the theatrical mechanics of an earlier age. But for all of Violet's irresistible biological energy, she too has social prejudices that reach into the past: twice, indeed, the subject of her marriage and pregnancy becomes an occasion for the ironic defusing of Tanner's radicalism. These lovers who outwit a disapproving parent are, in fact, what Tanner calls moral imposters, and both their ultimate conventionality and the perfunctory quality of the opposition they surmount cause us to reflect upon the sympathy that we normally give to characters in their place. So that here too, Shaw has cast both a cynical and an optimistic light on the convention—which, apparently dramatizing the rebellious triumph of the young, was really showing merely how "chance . . . achieved what the parents intended,"[12] but which also, in however hidden or distorted a way, bore the imprint of life's ultimate purpose.

The main plot of *Man and Superman* also reinterprets a familiar comic situation in a manner that seems, at first, entirely ironic. This is a play about a lively and amusing young man who enlists the aid of his comic servant and does everything else he can to *avoid* getting married—and fails. John Tanner seems to know more than anyone else on the stage about nearly everything except himself. His radical notions of free love, his unsentimental assessment of sexual attraction, evolution, and conventional morality are impressively laid out in his *Revolutionist's Handbook* and expounded in witty dialogue on the stage. But they avail him not in the end. "I am neither the slave of love nor its dupe," he says early in the play. But by the final scene, Tanner is himself tricked and trapped into marriage by the same Life Force whose stratagems he explains so well. Tanner's is the basic comic dilemma: his grand apprehension of the human situation fails to save him from—indeed, makes him vulnerable to—all sorts of specific, practical misapprehensions of the world around him. Again and again throughout the play he is deflated, belittled, and contradicted by events. "I hope you will be more careful in future about the things you say," says Violet after one such incident, "Of course, one does not take them seriously; but they are very disagreeable, and rather in bad taste, I think." The last lines of the play confirm this repeated joke and leave an enduring image of the would-be revolutionist encouraged to "go on talking" by his affectionate but uncomprehending lover while the rest of the cast join in "Universal laughter." For all the ironic distance between Tanner and his ancestors on the comic stage, his total situation finally takes on a strangely familiar shape. He is a beguiler beguiled, a moral terrorist hoist with his own petard; like our double image of Socrates, he is a universal *eiron* stranded in a world that calls him imposter.

But if, in enacting this familiar yet unusual comic story, Shaw beats the ironic comedians of his tradition at their own game, he also goes beyond to find "some truth or other behind all this frightful irony."[13] To appreciate the larger vision that Tanner's example also embodies, we need to consider the complex structure of the play that keeps him at center stage for nearly all of its considerable length. We have already noticed that Shaw attacked most subjects both in theatrical debate and in authorial monologue, and the total work *Man and Superman* comprises a play within a play within a book, inviting us to look, as it were, both inside and outside the central comic plot. In this, we sense the playwright grappling with the paradox of comic "realism," the basic dramatic ambiguity of mirror versus performance. At the heart of his "perfectly modern," apparently realistic three-act play, Shaw inserts a "totally extraneous act" in which characters drawn from a preexisting fiction meet to share an eloquent "Shavio-Socratic dialogue," which, as its author frankly admits, is thoroughly unsuitable for "immediate production." In its length and intellectual complexity, *Don Juan in Hell* disappoints the traditional expectations of performance, but at the same time, Shaw suggests that the serviceable comedy that frames it is no true "mirror" either—it is instead, as he describes it, merely a *"trumpery* story of modern London life."[14] Such modern stories, like comedy in general, usually end with a marriage—as this one does. But seen in this light, we can also conclude that the cynical, "realistic," and thoroughly comic conquest of John Tanner by Ann Whitefield and the Life Force is finally also an exigency of commercial playwriting, a concession to the traditions of fiction and theater. In another of those odd correspondences between life and art that we have met before, the ending of *Man and Superman* represents a possible capitulation to society-as-it-is by Bernard Shaw no less than by John Tanner. In traditional comedies, the audience implicitly demands a happy ending that its cynical common sense says is impractical and implausible; but here, our sympathy demands that an impractical idealist be brought down to earth in a comic resolution that proves him no different from ourselves.

Insofar as we agree with Ramsden that Tanner simply should get married "the sooner the better," *Man and Superman* is the portrayal of someone who, like the protagonists of Greek New Comedy and its imitators, struggles unaware against his own "imminent good fortune."[15] But I find the ending of this play to be happy in a larger sense. In the dream sequence of the third act, Shaw envisions Tanner *sub specie aeternitatis,* as a character from a past fiction speaking outside the realm of time. Thus Don Juan is Tanner as he "really" is—as purified of history as of our skepticism. Like Plato, Shaw is trying to embody in the rhythms of dialogue a truth that transcends both the fictional mirror and the moral illusions of real life. As Don Juan puts it, "If the play still goes on here and on earth, and all the world is a stage, heaven is at least behind the scenes." Still, Don Juan's ideas are Tanner's—elevated from the level of mere iconoclasm and impudent wit, to a fully developed, positive faith. Tanner, the turn-of-the-century gentleman-revolutionist, is at least one step more advanced on the evolutionary scale than his famous ancestor, the mere seducer and libertine portrayed by Tirso de Molina or Molière. In the same way, Don Juan, the eloquent spokesman for the Life Force, has taken the evolution of human consciousness even further. In their own contexts, all three were and are heralds of the Life to Come, members of the one true avant-garde. What we learn about the significance of human relationships in the dream sequence seems to transfigure the earthly story that it frames. As Don Juan describes the evolution of his own consciousness: "I had come to believe that I was a purely rational creature: a thinker! I said, with the foolish philosopher, 'I think: therefore I am.' It was Woman who taught me to say 'I am, therefore I think.' And also 'I would think more; therefore I must be more.' " So Tanner's irresistible attraction to Ann Whitefield demonstrates the validity as well as the comic inadequacy of his ideas. Tanner is, in other words, both more and less than he seems. As Shaw's work in general can still inspire us with a sense of responsibility to the future that transcends the difference between Darwin and Lamarck, so what we can learn from this infernal debate is, in the simplest terms, that we all contribute to the purpose of life by doing what we can.

Notice too, how the same joke which in the main play allows us to take Tanner as an impotent windbag is used, in the dream sequence, to opposite effect. Here, for example, is Tanner in act 1, carried away by his own rhetorical questions:

> TANNER. Are women taught better than men or worse? Are mobs of voters taught better than statesmen or worse? Worse, of course, in both cases. And then what sort of world are you going to get, with its public men considering its voting mobs, and its private men considering their wives? What does Church and State mean nowadays? The Woman and the Ratepayer.
>
> ANN (*placidly*). I am so glad you understand politics, Jack: it will be most useful to you if you go into parliament (*he collapses like a pricked bladder*).

In this exchange, Ann's complacence embodies the healthy inertia of the normal, the comic realism that, on the stage at least, always triumphs over professional and pedant. In hell, the same device of anticlimax makes us laugh for different reasons. Here, by contrast, is the beginning and the end of Don Juan's most magnificent speech (omitting several dozen pairs of opposite qualities):

> DON JUAN. Your friends are the dullest dogs I know. They are not beautiful: they are only decorated . . . not generous, only propitiatory; not disciplined, only cowed; and not truthful at all: liars every one of them, to the very backbone of their souls.
>
> THE STATUE. Your flow of words is simply amazing, Juan. . . .

This is not the pressure of the real breaking in on the rhetorical flight of a mere talker, but is rather a concession by the playwright to an imagined audience that cannot bear very much reality. The joke reveals that this magic mirror of thought and language is still a mere performance: but it also reminds us that the Pentecostal flame is still alight even though we are not always "strong enough to bear its terrible intensity."[16]

In the contrast between his mundane comedy and its philosophic core, Shaw illustrates the transcendent comic relationship between the individual destiny and the pattern of history. In our total apprehension of the play, Shaw's irony terminates in affirmation instead of negation. John Tanner the man, as his fictional ancestor and their common creator implicitly suggest, is no more limited and no less powerful than we are; his wit and energy, like Shaw's, are still part of life's process and progress, and they contain, we can be sure, "some truth or other." After the vision, even Tanner's histrionics take on a deeper significance:

> HECTOR. Miss Whitefield tracked you at every stopping place: she is a regular Sherlock Holmes.
>
> TANNER. The Life Force! I am lost!

If this is far funnier on the stage than the written words can possibly suggest, it is, I believe, because Tanner's little piece of self-mockery enacts the rhythms of life with that extraordinary brevity that, as Shakespeare and Freud alike realized, joins the techniques of wit with their real significance. Tanner is both lost and found: his comedy emerged from a father's death and an unexpected inheritance, and it ends with the painful discovery of the "father's heart" inside himself. In this sense, as with the other transcendent comedies we have considered, the real happy ending is "not yet."

Thus the comic hero of *Man and Superman,* to quote another critic's unimprovable summary, "remains in the hands of an artist who converts his defeat into a victory by ironizing it from start to finish."[17] We can also notice, without subscribing to the old critical complaint that Shaw's characters are all puppets set up to spout Shaw, that the author's presence does remain with us throughout this play. It is known, for example, that when Harley Granville-Barker played Tanner in the original production, his make-up was designed to recall the familiar bewhiskered features of GBS. Even more to the point is the parallel between Tanner's comic dilemma and Shaw's relationship with his audience. In the preface, conceding that his total design for *Man and Superman* goes beyond the practical limits of contemporary theater, Shaw admits that *"neither this epistle dedicatory* nor the dream of Don Juan . . . is suitable for immediate production."[18] Of course, he always liked to remind us that he was a bit of an actor himself, and that his public image was pure performance, but here, Shaw suggests specifically that the preface too is part of the "play." In it, the playwright makes us laugh at his own predicament with the same device of comic anticlimax that recurs so frequently in the main action:

> In vain do I redouble the violence of the language in which
> I proclaim my heterodoxies. I rail . . . at the stupid system of
> violence and robbery which we call Law and Industry. . . . And
> yet, instead of exclaiming "Send this inconceivable Satanist to
> the stake," the respectable newspapers pith me by announcing
> "another book by this brilliant and thoughtful writer."[19]

Like Tanner, Shaw has found the force of his onslaught "destroyed by a simple policy of non-resistance." Some spectators called him a brute and went about their business, while others looked on in rapt adoration and hung on every word, but they all said, in effect, "go on talking." Shaw's audience, critical or otherwise, has restored a Saturnalian quality to his comic vision. Believing that "heretical teaching must be made irresistibly attractive by fine art if the heretics are not to starve or burn,"[20] Shaw succeeded only too well in attracting audiences of "artistic people" who would ignore the teaching in their appreciation of the art. For their original spectators, Shaw's plays were a temporary indulgence in a shocking and titillating radicalism. To today's audiences, they can seem merely quaint and talky, resistant to modern production and varnished with excessive fame. Even his admirers seem to find in Shaw's plays only what he might have called a Thursday-to-Sunday holiday in the fool's paradise of art, in "that No Man's Land of luxuries for which there is nothing to pay, of poignant griefs that do not hurt, thrilling joys that do not satisfy, virtuous aspirations that do not ennoble, and fierce crusades that leave evil none the weaker, but rather the more prosperous for the advertisement."[21] One recent critic declares that "Shaw's statement that for art's sake alone he 'would not face the toil of writing a single sentence' is simply untrue."[22] The editor of a collection of essays on Shaw praises one of its contributors for his ability to analyze the Shavian dialectic "with a detachment so complete as to enable us to recognise it as dramatic style, artistic structuring."[23] Shaw has been, I believe, caught up in the paradox of comedy, his explosive ideas defused by the inevitable comic tendency to balance optimism with cynicism, utopian aspiration with ideological skepticism. After all, it was Shaw's own comic skill, his own self-chosen masks of Jester, Privileged Lunatic, witty and irascible GBS, that somehow licensed readers and audiences to enjoy him without responding seriously to his challenge. It was this professional talk maker's own finely tempered ironies that taught us the world cannot be saved by talk alone.

In some of his later comedies, correspondingly, Shaw tries to embody in his happy endings that union of wisdom and power that eluded him in his career. Thus the conventionally comic marriage of Adolphus Cusins, professor of Greek and translator of Euripides, to Major Barbara of the Salvation Army represents the coming-together of knowledge and faith—which, united, proceed to inherit the factory of power. Androcles' love for all living creatures allows him to saunter out of his play as a free man with an affectionate lion at his heels to keep the wolves at bay. The Millionairess, another embodiment of that soulless cunning and energy that Shaw at least partly admired, finally marries the Egyptian doctor, a stock figure of impractical altruism, a Man with a Purpose. Even as Shaw's dramatic craftsmanship grew more perfunctory, his audience more complacent, his specific causes less relevant, the faith that he continued to express in the ancient patterns of comedy still defined his triumph over the critical imposters and an increasingly disastrous world picture. I must preach and preach, no matter how late the day, says a late Shavian character: the message will be heard again, like laughter. And now, on the other side of Shaw's solutions and resolutions, the comic spirit advances further into absurdity and television, or retreats into the cosmic gallows humor of Samuel Beckett—whose real comic target is life itself and who can teach us no more consoling way to "magnify the Almighty than by sniggering with him at his little jokes, particularly the poorer ones."[24] But Shaw continues to ask us (in a rhetorical question that unites comedy's value, purpose, and form in one more illuminating paradox), "Suppose the world *were* only one of God's jokes: would you work any the less to make it a good joke instead of a bad one?"[25]

Notes

Chapter 1 Character

1 *Pseudolus,* in *Plautus,* trans. Paul Nixon, Loeb Classical Library (London: William Heinemann Ltd., 1932), 4:227–28.

2 Henri Bergson, *Laughter* (1900); reprinted in *Comedy,* ed. Wylie Sypher (Garden City, N.Y.: Doubleday Anchor Books, 1956), p. 61.

3 Sigmund Freud, *Jokes and Their Relation to the Unconscious,* trans. James Strachey (New York: W. W. Norton and Co., 1960), p. 155.

4 Ibid., p. 49.

5 The first phrase is from Ralph Waldo Emerson's "Comedy," in *The Early Lectures of Ralph Waldo Emerson,* ed. Robert E. Spiller and Wallace E. Williams (Cambridge: Harvard University Press, Belknap Press, 1972), 3:123. The second phrase is from Aristotle's *Poetics* 5.1, in *Aristotle's Theory of Poetry and Fine Art,* trans. S. H. Butcher (New York: St. Martin's Press, 1954). All subsequent references to the *Poetics* will be to this edition.

6 L. J. Potts, *Comedy* (London: Hutchinson's University Library, n.d.), p. 19.

7 Leo Salingar, *Shakespeare and the Traditions of Comedy* (Cambridge: Cambridge University Press, 1974), p. 7.

8 W. K. Wimsatt, "Aristotle and Oedipus or Else," in *Hateful Contraries: Studies in Literature and Criticism* (Lexington: University of Kentucky Press, 1974), p. 74.

9 Translated by Paul Shorey in *The Collected Dialogues of Plato,* ed. Edith Hamilton and Huntington Cairns, Bollingen Series 71 (Princeton: Princeton University Press, 1961), p. 831.

10 Hamilton and Cairns, *Collected Dialogues,* trans. A. E. Taylor, p. 1386.

11 Translated by Benjamin Jowett, *The Basic Works of Aristotle,* ed. Richard McKeon (New York: Random House, 1941), p. 1304.

12 Hamilton and Cairns, *Collected Dialogues,* trans. R. Hackforth, p. 1129.

13 *Menander: The Principal Fragments,* ed. and trans. Francis G. Allinson, Loeb Classical Library (London: William Heinemann Ltd., 1930), p. xiii.

14 All quotations from Horace are from *Satires, Epistles and Ars Poetica,* ed. and

trans. H. Rushton Fairclough, Loeb Classical Library (London: William Heinemann Ltd., 1920).

15 Ovid, *Heroides and Amores*, trans. Grant Showerman, Loeb Classical Library (London: William Heinemann Ltd., 1926), 1:377.

16 *Elizabethan Critical Essays*, ed. G. Gregory Smith (Oxford: Clarendon Press, 1904), 1:60.

17 *Miscellaneous Prose of Sir Philip Sidney*, ed. Katherine Duncan-Jones and Jan Van Dorsten (Oxford: Clarendon Press, 1973), p. 96.

18 G. Blakemore Evans, ed., in *The Plays of George Chapman: The Comedies*, ed. Alan Holaday (Urbana: University of Illinois Press, 1970), p. 262. Reference is to act, scene, and lines.

19 *The Complete Plays of William Wycherley*, ed. Gerald Weales (New York: New York University Press, 1967), p. 266. Reference is to act and scene.

20 The definition is preserved in Donatus, *De Comoedia* 5.1, in *Aeli Donati Commentum Terenti*, ed. Paulus Wessner (Leipzig: B. G. Teubneri, 1902), 1:22.

21 Allan H. Gilbert, *Literary Criticism: Plato to Dryden* (New York: American Book Company, 1940), p. 225.

22 Frederick Morgan Padelford, *Select Translations from Scaliger's Poetics*, Yale Studies in English 36 (New York: Henry Holt and Co., 1905), p. 39.

23 Gilbert, *Literary Criticism*, p. 330.

24 Charles Sterrett Latham, *A Translation of Dante's Eleven Letters* (Cambridge, Mass.: Riverside Press, 1891), p. 197.

25 Aristophanes, *Acharnians*, trans. B. B. Rogers Loeb, in *The Complete Plays of Aristophanes*, ed. Moses Hadas (New York: Bantam Books, 1962), p. 29.

26 Juvenal, *Satires* 3:152–53, in *Juvenal and Persius*, trans. G. B. Ramsay, Loeb Classical Library (London: William Heinemann Ltd., 1918), p. 42.

Chapter 2   Plot

1 *The Works of Charles Lamb*, ed. Thomas Hutchinson (Oxford: Oxford University Press, 1924), p. 648.

2 See, for example, Northrop Frye, *Anatomy of Criticism* (Princeton: Princeton University Press, 1957), p. 171; and C. L. Barber, *Shakespeare's Festive Comedy: A Study of Dramatic Form and Its Relation to Social Custom* (Princeton: Princeton University Press, 1959), pp. 7–15.

3 Ian Donaldson, *The World Upside Down: Comedy from Jonson to Fielding* (Oxford: Clarendon Press, 1970), p. 14.

4 Charles Sterrett Latham, *A Translation of Dante's Eleven Letters* (Cambridge, Mass.: Riverside Press, 1891), p. 197.

5 Frederick Morgan Padelford, *Select Translations from Scaliger's Poetics*, Yale Studies in English 36 (New York: Henry Holt and Co., 1905), p. 39.

6 Donatus, *Evanthus de Fabula, Aeli Donati Commentum Terenti*, ed. Paulus Wessner (Leipzig: B. G. Teubneri, 1902), 1.21.

7 *A Midsummer Night's Dream* 3.2.461–62. All quotations from Shakespeare are from *The Riverside Shakespeare*, ed. G. Blakemore Evans (Boston: Houghton Mifflin Co., 1974).

8 Donatus, *Aeli Donati Commentum Terenti*, 1:22.

9 Ben Jonson, *Works*, ed. C. H. Herford and Percy Simpson and Evelyn Simpson (Oxford: Clarendon Press, 1925–52), 6:578.

10 Franciscus Robortellus, *On Comedy* (1548), trans. Marvin T. Herrick, in Herrick, *Comic Theory in the Sixteenth Century* (Urbana: University of Illinois Press, 1950), p. 232.

11 Wylie Sypher, "The Meanings of Comedy," afterword in *Comedy*, ed. Wylie Sypher (Garden City, N.Y.: Doubleday Anchor Books, 1956), p. 219.

12 Cicero, *Ad Herennium*, trans. Harry Caplan, Loeb Classical Library (London: William Heinemann Ltd., 1954), pp. 24–25.

13 H. B. Charlton, *Castelvetro's Theory of Poetry* (Manchester: Manchester University Press, 1913), p. 136.

14 Herrick, *Comic Theory in the Sixteenth Century*, p. 123.

15 Bernardino Daniello, *Poetics* (1536), trans. Lander MacClintock, in *European Theories of the Drama*, ed. Barrett H. Clark (New York: Crown Publishers, 1918), p. 41. Cf. Horace, *Ars Poetica* 191–92.

16 Euripides, *Helen* (1689–92), trans. Richmond Lattimore, *The Complete Greek Tragedies*, ed. David Grene and Richmond Lattimore (Chicago: University of Chicago Press, 1959). There is some debate as to whether Euripides intended these lines to appear in all the plays.

17 All quotations from Gay are from *The Beggar's Opera*, ed. Peter Fled Lewis (Edinburgh: Oliver and Boyd, 1973).

18 Bertolt Brecht, *The Threepenny Opera*, trans. Desmond Vesey and Eric Bentley (New York: Grove Press, 1949), p. 96.

Chapter 3   From Irony to Transcendence

1 Henri Bergson, *Laughter* (1900); reprinted in *Comedy*, ed. Wylie Sypher (Garden City, N.Y.: Doubleday Anchor Books, 1956), p. 148.

2 "Vexed all the while with two talking ladies and Sir. Ch. Sidley, yet pleased to hear their discourse . . . a more pleasant recontre I never heard. But by that means lost the pleasure of the play wholly" (February 18, 1667, *The Diary of Samuel Pepys*, ed. Robert Latham and William Matthews [Berkeley: University of California Press, 1974], 4:71–72).

3 William Congreve, *Letters and Documents*, ed. John C. Hodges (New York: Harcourt, Brace and World, 1964), p. 181.

4 Mikhail Bakhtin, *Rabelais and His World*, trans. Helen Iswolsky (Cambridge: MIT Press, 1968), p. 90.

5 Ernst Bloch, *A Philosophy of the Future*, trans. John Cumming (New York: Herder and Herder, 1970), p. 92.

6 I use, in this one instance, the translation by Benjamin Jowett, *The Dialogues of Plato* (New York: Charles Scribner's Sons, 1907).

7 The definition of comic *katharsis* comes from the so-called *Tractatus Coislinianus*, originally printed by J. A. Cramer in his *Anecdota Graeca* (1839). See Lane Cooper, *An Aristotelian Theory of Comedy* (New York: Harcourt, Brace and Co., 1922), p. 10.

8 *The Works of Charles Lamb*, ed. Thomas Hutchinson (Oxford: Oxford University Press, 1924), pp. 649–50.

9 Ian Donaldson, *The World Upside Down: Comedy from Jonson to Fielding* (Oxford: Clarendon Press, 1970), p. 10.

10 Elmer Edgar Stoll, *Shakespeare Studies* (New York: G. E. Stechert and Co., 1942), p. 52.

11 Albert Cook, *The Dark Voyage and the Golden Mean* (Cambridge: Harvard University Press, 1949), p. 45.

12 Ortega y Gassett, *Meditations on Quixote*, trans. Evelyn Rugg and Diego Marin (New York: W. W. Norton and Co., 1961), p. 158.

13 Samuel Johnson, *Lives of the English Poets*, ed. George Birkbeck Hill (Oxford: Clarendon Press, 1905), 2:22.

14 Bakhtin, *Rabelais and His World*, p. 90.

15 Sigmund Freud, *Jokes and Their Relation to the Unconscious*, trans. James Strachey (New York: W. W. Norton and Co., 1960), p. 105.

16 George Thomson, *Aeschylus and Athens: A Study in the Social Origins of Drama* (London: Lawrence and Wishart, 1941), pp. 359–60.

17 Freud, *Jokes*, pp. 110–11.

18 Thomas Middleton, *No Wit, No Help Like a Woman's*, 1.2.1–3, in *The Works of Thomas Middleton*, ed. A. H. Bullen (Boston: Houghton Mifflin and Co., 1885), p. 297.

19 John Kenneth Galbraith, *Money: Whence It Came, Where It Went* (Boston: Houghton Mifflin Co., 1975), p. 62.

20 Plautus, *The Comedy of Asses*, 1.3.173–75, in *Plautus*, trans. Paul Nixon, Loeb Classical Library (London: William Heinemann Ltd., 1932), 1:143.

21 William Wycherley, *The Plain Dealer*, Prologue, in *Complete Plays*, ed. Gerald Weales (New York: New York University Press, 1967), p. 386.

22 Ludovico Ariosto, *Lena*, trans. Guy William, in *Five Italian Renaissance Comedies*, ed. Bruce Penman (Penguin Books, 1978), p. 67.

23 Northrop Frye, *Anatomy of Criticism* (Princeton: Princeton University Press, 1957), p. 163.

24 *Back to Methusaleh*, in *The Bodley Head Bernard Shaw* (London: Max Reinhardt, 1972), 5:345.

Chapter 4   The Plautine Success Story

1 *Major Barbara*, Preface, in *The Bodley Head Bernard Shaw* (London: Max Reinhardt, 1972), 3:31.

2 "A Defense of Poetry," *Miscellaneous Prose of Sir Philip Sidney*, ed. Katherine Duncan-Jones and Jan Van Dorsten (Oxford: Clarendon Press, 1973), pp. 95–96.

3 Henri Bergson, *Laughter* (1900), reprinted in *Comedy*, ed. Wylie Sypher (Garden City, N.Y.: Doubleday Anchor Books, 1956), p. 148.

4 Raymond Williams, *Keywords: A Vocabulary of Culture and Society* (New York: Oxford University Press, 1976), pp. 143–44.

5 Quoted by Edward Arber in his introduction to Stephen Gosson, *The School of Abuse* (London: Alex Murray and Son, 1868), p. 9.

6 E. K. Chambers, *The Elizabethan Stage* (Oxford: Clarendon Press, 1923), 1:348.

7 All quotations from Horace in this chapter are from *Horace: Satires, Epistles*

and Ars Poetica, ed. and trans. H. Rushton Fairclough, Loeb Classical Library
(London: William Heinemann Ltd., 1920). Reference is to line numbers of the
original Latin verse.

8 Gilbert Norwood, *Plautus and Terence* (New York: Longman's Green and
Co., 1932), p. 27 (my emphasis).

9 T. S. Eliot, "Tradition and the Individual Talent," in *Selected Essays* (London:
Faber and Faber, 1932), p. 21.

10 W. Beare agrees that "if Plautus' work was governed by practical considera-
tions . . . he seems at least to have taken some pride in his achievement" (*The
Roman Stage* [London: Methuen, 1950], p. 53). Erich Segal points out, "One
of the few indisputable statements which can be made about Plautus the man is
that he enjoyed great popular success" (*Roman Laughter: The Comedy of
Plautus* [Cambridge: Harvard University Press, 1968], p. 2).

11 *The Attic Nights of Aulus Gellius*, trans. John C. Rolfe, Loeb Classical Library
(New York: G. P. Putnam's Sons, 1927), p. 251. For a summary of the scholarly controversy surrounding this passage, see George Duckworth, *The Nature
of Roman Comedy* (Princeton: Princeton University Press, 1952), pp. 49–51.

12 *Periceiromene*, prologue 209, *Menander: The Principal Fragments*, ed. and
trans. Francis G. Allinson, Loeb Classical Library (London: William
Heinemann Ltd., 1930).

13 *Aeli Donati Commentum Terenti*, ed. Paulus Wessner (Leipzig: B. G.
Teubneri, 1902), 1:20.

14 All quotations from Plautus in this chapter are from the Loeb Classical Library
edition (London: William Heinemann Ltd., 1932–1937), the translations
slightly modified and modernized from those of Paul Nixon. References are to
line numbers of the Latin original.

15 See Marvin T. Herrick, *Tragicomedy: Its Origins and Development in Italy,
France and England* (Urbana: University of Illinois Press, 1955).

16 Bergson, *Comedy*, p. 97.

17 Paul Shaner Dunkin, *Post Aristophantic Comedy*, Illinois Studies in Language
and Literature 31 (Urbana: University of Illinois Press, 1946), p. 103.

18 Norwood, *Plautus and Terence*, p. 7.

19 Dunkin, *Post Aristophantic Comedy*, p. 103.

20 Segal, *Roman Laughter*, pp. 152, 160.

21 Sigmund Freud, "Humour," trans. Joan Riviere, *International Journal of
Psycho-Analysis* 9 (1928); reprinted in *Character and Culture*, ed. Philip Rief
(New York: Collier Books, 1963), p. 265.

Chapter 5   Machiavellian Humor

1 Gilbert Norwood, *Plautus and Terence* (New York: Longman's Green and
Co., 1932), p. 4.

2 Mikhail Bakhtin, *Rabelais and His World*, trans. Helen Iswolsky (Cambridge:
MIT Press, 1968), p. 24.

3 *Machiavelli: The Chief Works and Others*, trans. Alan Gilbert (Durham,
N.C.: Duke University Press, 1965), 2:902. All quotations from Machiavelli
are taken from this volume of this edition. References to *Mandragola* will be to
act and scene.

4 Ibid., pp. 1013–14.
5 See Robert Ridolfi, *The Life of Niccolò Machiavelli*, trans. Cecil Grayson (Chicago: University of Chicago Press, 1963).
6 Familiar letter, April 16, 1514, Machiavelli, *Works*, p. 943.
7 Familiar letter, June 10, 1514, ibid., p. 945.
8 Ridolfi, *Life of Machiavelli*, p. 169.
9 Ridolfi argues "If . . . there were a purpose behind it, one could hardly say that this was to make people laugh when the comedy has far more the effect of making people think" (ibid., p. 172). But John Addington Symonds asserts that "of satire or moral purpose there is none in the *Mandragola*" (*Renaissance Italy* [London: Smith, Elder and Co., 1881], 5:170).
10 Sydney Anglo, *Machiavelli: A Dissection* (London: Victor Gollancz, 1969), p. 203.
11 Marvin Herrick, *Italian Comedy in the Renaissance* (Urbana: University of Illinois Press, 1960), p. 81.
12 Ligurio tells Callimaco, "I'm saying that if you keep your spirits up and trust in me, I'll finish this business for you before tomorrow at this time" (1:3). When night falls, Frate Timoteo explains, "And you, spectators, don't find fault with us, because all night nobody here will get any sleep, so that acts aren't separated in time for it" (4:10)—a comically subjective view of the unity of time.
13 Leo Salingar, *Shakespeare and the Traditions of Comedy* (Cambridge: Cambridge University Press, 1974), p. 84.
14 "No comedy is so convincingly realistic . . ." (Herrick, *Italian Comedy*, p. 81).
15 John Wilmot, Earl of Rochester, "A Satyr against Reason and Mankind," *The Complete Poems*, ed. David M. Vieth (New Haven: Yale University Press, 1968), p. 100.
16 Elmer Edgar Stoll, *Shakespeare Studies* (New York: G. E. Stechert and Co., 1942), p. 183.
17 Symonds, *Renaissance Italy*, p. 169.
18 Bertolt Brecht, *Mother Courage and Her Children*, English version by Eric Bentley (New York: Grove Press, 1966), p. 61.

Chapter 6 Middleton's Trick

1 E. K. Chambers, *The Elizabethan Stage* (Oxford: Clarendon Press, 1923), 1:308.
2 Quoted by Edward Arber in his introduction to Stephen Gosson, *The School of Abuse* (London: Alex Murray and Son, 1868), p. 9.
3 Gosson, *School of Abuse*, p. 36.
4 Chambers, *Elizabethan Stage*, 1:259.
5 Ibid., pp. 350, 359 n. 1.
6 George Bernard Shaw, *Everybody's Political What's What?* (New York: Dodd, Mead and Co., 1944), p. 186.
7 All quotations from Shakespeare in this chapter are from *The Riverside Shakespeare*, ed. G. Blakemore Evans (Boston: Houghton Mifflin Co., 1974).
8 George Bernard Shaw, *Misalliance, The Dark Lady of the Sonnets, and Fanny's First Play* (London: Constable and Co., 1910), p. 242.
9 *Dark Lady of the Sonnets*, Preface, p. 212.

10 Sidney Lee, *A Life of William Shakespeare* (New York: Macmillan, 1909), p. 288.

11 See Alfred Harbage, *Conceptions of Shakespeare* (Cambridge: Harvard University Press, 1967), p. 11.

12 C. J. Ribton-Turner, *History of Vagrants and Vagrancy* (Chapman and Hall, 1887; reprint ed., Montclair, N.J.: Patterson Smith, 1972), p. 72.

13 Ben Jonson, *Works*, ed. C. H. Herford and Percy Simpson and Evelyn Simpson (Oxford: Clarendon Press, 1925–52), 1:57.

14 *Timber,* or *Discoveries,* ibid., 8:644.

15 "To the Worthy Author John Fletcher," ibid., p. 370.

16 Prologue, *Every Man in His Humour,* revised version 1616, ibid., 3:303.

17 Conversations with William Drummond of Hawthornden, ibid., 1:137.

18 Quoted by Kenneth Muir, introduction, Thomas Middleton, *Three Plays* (London: J. M. Dent and Sons, 1975), p. vii, and frequently elsewhere.

19 T. S. Eliot, "Thomas Middleton," in *Selected Essays* (London: Faber and Faber, 1932), pp. 169–70.

20 Dorothy M. Farr, *Thomas Middleton and the Drama of Realism* (Edinburgh: Oliver and Boyd, 1973), p. 6.

21 Eliot, *Selected Essays,* p. 167.

22 Thomas Middleton, *Michaelmas Term,* ed. George R. Price (The Hague: Mouton, 1976).

23 Thomas Middleton, *A Trick to Catch the Old One,* ed. Charles Barber, Fountainwell Drama Texts (Berkeley: University of California Press, 1968). All quotations from this play are from this edition. Reference is to act, scene, and lines.

24 Roger Manvell, *Chaplin* (Boston: Little, Brown, 1974), p. 68.

25 Northrop Frye, *Anatomy of Criticism* (Princeton: Princeton University Press, 1957), pp. 180–81.

26 R. B. Parker, "Middleton's Experiments with Comedy and Judgement," in *Jacobean Theatre,* ed. John Russel Brown and Bernard Harris (New York: Capricorn Books, 1960), p. 188.

27 George R. Rowe, Jr., *Thomas Middleton and the New Comedy Tradition* (Lincoln: University of Nebraska Press, 1979), p. 76.

28 David Holmes, *The Art of Thomas Middleton* (Oxford: Clarendon Press, 1970), p. 80.

29 Ibid., p. 81.

30 George Price, *Michaelmas Term,* p. 215.

31 T. S. Eliot, *Selected Essays,* p. 167.

32 Richard Hindry Barker, *Thomas Middleton* (New York: Columbia University Press, 1958), p. 46.

33 Parker, "Middleton's Experiments," p. 199.

Chapter 7   The Play and the World

1 All quotations from Euripides are in Richmond Lattimore's translation, from *The Complete Greek Tragedies,* ed. Richmond Lattimore and David Grene (Chicago: University of Chicago Press, 1955), vol. 3.

2 The phrase is Lattimore's, ibid., p. 485.

3 This famous comparison is preserved in Aristotle's *Poetics* (25.6).

4 George Meredith, *An Essay on Comedy and the Uses of the Comic Spirit* (London: Constable and Co., 1919), p. 88.

5 Wylie Sypher, "The Meanings of Comedy," in *Comedy,* ed. Wylie Sypher (Garden City, N.Y.: Doubleday Anchor Books, 1956), pp. 228–29.

6 Meredith, *Essay on Comedy,* p. 91.

7 John Dryden, "Defense of the Epilogue, or an Essay on the Dramatic Poets of the Last Age," in *Of Dramatic Poesy and Other Critical Essays,* ed. George Watson (London: L. M. Dent, 1962).

8 Goethe made this comment on the *Histoire de la vie des ouvrages de Molière,* by J. Taschereau, quoted in Fred O. Nolte, *The Early Middle Class Drama* (Lancaster, Pa.: Lancaster Press, 1935), p. 80.

9 Sypher, "The Meanings of Comedy," p. 255.

10 F. M. Cornford, *The Origins of Attic Comedy* (London: Edward Arnold, 1914), p. viii.

11 Northrop Frye, "The Argument of Comedy," in *English Institute Essays 1948,* ed. D. A. Robertson, Jr. (New York: Columbia University Press, 1949; reprint ed., New York: AMS Press, 1965), pp. 64–65.

12 Sigmund Freud, *Beyond the Pleasure Principle,* trans. James Strachey (New York: W. W. Norton and Co., 1961), pp. 8–9.

13 Ibid., p. 11.

14 T. W. Baldwin, *Shakespere's Five-Act Structure* (Urbana: University of Illinois Press, 1947), p. 112.

15 To be more specific, Donatus points out that the slave Davus narrates the heroine's story about her birth but expresses his own cynical disbelief of it, so that *abrogatur fides,* that is, we are also led to disbelieve it (*Aeli Donati Commentum Terenti,* ed. Paulus Wessner [Leipzig: B. G. Teubneri, 1902], 1:97).

16 Freud, *Beyond the Pleasure Principle,* p. 33.

17 *Heartbreak House,* act 2, *The Bodley Head Bernard Shaw* (London: Max Reinhardt, 1972), 5:146.

18 John Maxwell Edmonds, ed. and trans., *Fragments of Attic Comedy* (Leiden: E. J. Brill, 1959), 2:479.

19 All quotations from Beckett are taken from *Endgame: A Play in One Act* (New York: Grove Press, 1958).

Chapter 8   Medieval Mastery

1 Henri Bergson, *Laughter* (1900), reprinted in *Comedy,* ed. Wylie Sypher (Garden City, N.Y.: Doubleday Anchor Books, 1956), p. 190.

2 Ernst Bloch, *A Philosophy of the Future,* trans. John Cumming (New York: Herder and Herder, 1970), pp. 94–95.

3 George Bernard Shaw, *John Bull's Other Island,* act 4, in *The Bodley Head Bernard Shaw* (London: Max Reinhardt, 1972), 2:1021.

4 *Periceiromene,* prologue 209, *Menander: The Principal Fragments,* ed. and trans. Francis G. Allinson, Loeb Classical Library (London: William Heinemann Ltd., 1930).

5   E. K. Chambers, *The Mediaeval Stage* (Oxford: Clarendon Press, 1903), 2:147.
6   Ibid., p. 139.
7   Ibid., p. 110.
8   F. M. Salter, *Mediaeval Drama in Chester* (Toronto: University of Toronto Press, 1955), p. 53.
9   All quotations from the Wakefield Master are from *The Wakefield Pageants in the Townley Cycle*, ed. A. C. Cawley (Manchester: Manchester University Press, 1958).
10 *Epitrepontes*, in *Menander: Principal Fragments*, p. 121.
11 See William Makepeace Thackeray, *The Book of Snobs*, in *The Works of William Makepeace Thackeray* (London: Smith, Elder and Co., 1899), 6:303.
12 There is some controversy as to the meaning of "frerys," which is usually taken to be in apposition to "begars" as referring to mendicant friars. This enigmatic reference may be another example of the Wakefield Master's contemporary satire. The precise nature of the beggars, however, does not affect the scene's emotional point.

Chapter 9   Mayakovsky's Mystery

1   *The Complete Plays of Vladimir Mayakovsky*, trans. Guy Daniels (New York: Simon and Schuster, 1968), p. 32. All quotations from Mayakovsky are from this edition.
2   Lewis S. Feuer, introduction, in Karl Marx and Frederick Engels, *Basic Writings in Politics and Philosophy*, ed. Lewis Feuer (Garden City, N.Y.: Doubleday and Co., 1968), p. xi.
3   Karl Marx and Frederick Engels, *The Communist Manifesto* (1888), in ibid., p. 29.
4   *Syevyernaya Kommuna*, October 12, 1918, signed by Meyerhold, Mayakovsky, and others, cited by Wiktor Woroszylski, in *The Life of Mayakovsky*, trans. Boleslaw Taborski (New York: Orion Press, 1970), p. 237.
5   Ibid., pp. 237–38.
6   Ibid., p. 240.
7   Ibid., p. 238.
8   Maynard Solomon, *Marxism and Art: Essays Classic and Contemporary* (New York: Vintage Books, 1974), p. 241.
9   Ibid.
10 Woroszylski, *Life of Mayakovsky*, p. 241.
11 Edward J. Brown, *Mayakovsky, A Poet in the Revolution* (Princeton: Princeton University Press, 1973), p. 200.
12 George Bernard Shaw, *Man and Superman*, Preface, in *The Bodley Head Bernard Shaw* (London: Max Reinhardt, 1972), 2:497.
13 F. M. Cornford, *The Origins of Attic Comedy* (London: Edward Arnold, 1914), p. viii.

Chapter 10   The Shavian Solution

1   *Back to Methusaleh,* part 1: "In the Beginning," act 1, in *The Bodley Head Bernard Shaw* (London: Max Reinhardt, 1972), 5:349. Unless otherwise noted, all quotations from Shaw will be from this edition, identified by volume and page.

2   Ibid., 5:335–36.

3   Irving Wardle, "The Plays," in *The Genius of Shaw: A Symposium,* ed. Michael Holroyd (New York: Holt, Rinehart and Winston, 1979), p. 149.

4   The first phrases are from the preface to *Man and Superman,* 2:523; the latter from *Back to Methusaleh,* "Postscript: After Twenty-Five Years," 5:692.

5   George Bernard Shaw, *Everybody's Political What's What?* (New York: Dodd, Mead and Co., 1944), p. 190.

6   Preface, *Heartbreak House,* 5:56; Preface, *Man and Superman,* 2:495.

7   "Who I Am and What I Think," part 2, *The Candid Friend,* May 18, 1901, quoted by Eric Bentley in *Bernard Shaw* (London: Robert Hale Ltd., 1950), p. 209.

8   Clarence Rook, *The Chap Book,* November 1, 1896, p. 539, quoted by Eric Bentley, ibid.

9   Alick West, "*A Good Man Fallen Among Fabians,*" (London: Lawrence and Wishart, 1950), p. 54.

10 Preface, *Man and Superman,* 2:518.

11 *The Self Tormentor,* in *Terence,* trans. John Sargeaunt, Loeb Classical Library (London: William Heinemann Ltd., 1953), 1:136.

12 Molière, *Les Fourberies de Scapin,* in *The Miser and Other Plays,* trans. John Wood (Penguin Books, 1953), p. 104.

13 *Major Barbara,* act 3, 3:156.

14 Preface, *Man and Superman,* 2:504 (my emphasis).

15 Leo Salingar, *Shakespeare and the Traditions of Comedy* (Cambridge: Cambridge University Press, 1974), p. 84.

16 *Too True to be Good,* 6:528.

17 Wardle, "The Plays," p. 156.

18 Preface, *Man and Superman,* 2:518 (my emphasis).

19 Ibid., p. 525.

20 *Back to Methusaleh,* "Postscript: After Twenty-Five Years," 5:695.

21 George Bernard Shaw, "Ouida's Successor," *Paul Mall Gazette,* June 29, 1887, in *Bernard Shaw's Non-Dramatic Literary Criticism,* ed. Stanley Weintraub (Lincoln: University of Nebraska Press, 1972), p. 35.

22 J. I. M. Stewart, *Eight Modern Writers* (Oxford: Clarendon Press, 1963), p. 126.

23 Rose Zimbardo, Introduction to *Twentieth Century Interpretations of Major Barbara,* ed. Rose Zimbardo (New York: Prentice-Hall, 1970), p. 2.

24 Samuel Beckett, *Happy Days: A Play* (New York: Grove Press, 1961), p. 31.

25 Letter to Leo Tolstoy, February 14, 1910, George Bernard Shaw, *Collected Letters 1898–1910,* ed. Dan H. Laurence (New York: Dodd, Mead and Co., 1972), p. 902.

Index

Aeschylus, 89
Anglo, Sidney, 56
Ariosto, *Lena*, 32
Aristophanes, 13 n. 25, 33, 45
    Aristophanic *alazon*, 93
    Aristophanic *eiron*, 11, 93
Aristotle, 5, 20, 24, 28, 94
    doctrine of *katharsis*, 28
    Poetics, 6–7, 9, 12–13, 18, 19
    Politics, 8, 9

Bakhtin, Mikhail, 30, 53, 85, 113
Barker, Richard Hindry, 84–85 n. 32
Beckett, Samuel, 99–102, 137
    Endgame, 99–102
Benny, Jack, 37
Bergson, Henri, 3, 24, 38, 39, 42, 48, 103
    Le Rire, 38
Bloch, Ernst, 103, 116
Brecht, Bertolt, 24, 50, 65
    Threepenny Opera, 24

Castelvetro, Lodovico, 13, 19
Chambers, E. K., 67, 106
Chaplin, Charlie, 30, 77
    The Great Dictator, 30
Chapman, George, *All Fooles*, 11
Cicero, 12, 15, 19
Coleridge, Samuel Taylor, 118

Collier, Jeremy, *Short View of the English Stage*, 29
Comedy of manners, 37, 74
Congreve, Samuel, 26
Cook, Albert, 29
Cornford, F. M., 96
Corpus Christi plays, 104–15, 118
    Chester Cycle, 106
    Townley Cycle, 106

Daniello, Bernadino, 20
Dante, 13, 17, 104, 110
Decorum, doctrine of, 9
Dekker, Thomas, 70
Donaldson, Ian, 16, 29 n. 9
Donatus the Grammarian, 17, 18, 44, 98
Dryden, John, 95, 98
Dunkin, Paul, 48, 51

Eliot, T. S., 42, 75, 84
Euripides, 20–21, 89–93, 113
    Alcestis, 92
    Helen, 89–93, 95, 110

Fielding, Henry, 14, 47
Fields, W. C., 3, 25, 57, 108
Freud, Sigmund, 3, 4–5, 30, 31, 51–52, 96–97, 98, 134
Frye, Northrop, 33, 80